To: Eric & Sharon

From: Henry H. Funk

The old vision restated
with power and inspiration!
A great book. Wanted you
to have a copy. Has much
to say about the validity
of the mission of North
Star Mennonite and Bethany
Mennonite — as well as
its preachers!

God Bless!

THE
VALIDITY
OF THE
CHRISTIAN
MISSION

The
VALIDITY
of the
CHRISTIAN
MISSION

Elton Trueblood

PROFESSOR-AT-LARGE
EARLHAM COLLEGE

HARPER & ROW, PUBLISHERS

New York, Evanston, San Francisco, London

To My Friends
at Kaimosi in Kenya

Contents

Preface

In my earlier years it did not occur to me that I might write a book on the Christian Mission. Though I was influenced in my youth by the Student Volunteer Movement, and though I read those who interpreted the missionary phenomenon convincingly, the possibility that I ought to try to write on the subject did not even enter my mind. What finally made the difference was the opportunity of firsthand observation of the World Mission, particularly in a slow world tour beginning in November 1970. In many areas I met people who have emerged from barbarism in two generations, the emergence occurring chiefly because of Christian people who have served other people as Christ's representatives. I saw hospitals which would never have existed apart from the generosity of thousands of humble donors and hundreds of anonymous workers.

One day, as I was riding in a car near Nairobi, the decision to write was suddenly formed. As the wonder of the Mission burst upon me, I saw that the idea of Mission, far from being something peripheral or incidental to the Christian faith, is actually the factor which brings the entire Christian Cause into focus. Now I see that in my public career I have been approaching the uniting idea of Mission for a long time and from a variety of angles. Though I did not realize it earlier, this is what I have been trying to say in most of my books, including even the philosophical ones. The closest connection, however, is with *The Future of the Christian* in that the present volume expands some of the ideas introduced there.

What do we mean by a missionary? The term is not limited to a profession, as it is not limited to the work of Church boards. A missionary is anyone who serves as a consequence of being profoundly touched by the love of Christ. The validity of this conception has little to do with geography. If it is not valid on the foreign field, it will turn out to be invalid at home. And the notion that we can keep the remainder of Christianity with the Mission deleted is one in which there is no validity at all.

Noble as the missionary enterprise has been, there is no doubt that today it is in serious danger, for many of the people who once believed in it now believe in it no more. What they require, and what they have a right to expect, is intellectual justification. What is widely doubted is not some detail of the Christian Mission or some denominational program, but the entire conception. Some are called, consequently, to participate in the process of validation. The urgent question is not whether missionary hospitals and schools should be nationalized or whether we should concentrate on work at home rather than abroad, but whether the basic idea itself is a sound one. This is the question which many are now asking and about which they deserve a thoughtful answer.

Many books suffer from their authors' overnumerous intentions, but, fortunately, the present book has only one purpose. I am trying to take seriously the doubts which honest and goodhearted people have today as they question whether the Christian Mission has any contemporary justification. I write because I believe that such justification is possible and that a clear affirmative answer can be given. As I write, I keep thinking of the words of I Peter 3:15: "Always be prepared to make a defense to any one who calls you to account for the hope that is in you, yet do it with gentleness and reverence." Someone must provide this defense, not only with gentleness and reverence, but also with intellectual integrity.

E.T.

Earlham College
August 1971

THE
VALIDITY
OF THE
CHRISTIAN
MISSION

1

The Phenomenon
of Mission

> Let all nations hear the sound by word or
> writing.
>
> GEORGE FOX

The Christian Mission is an astonishing phenomenon. A particular movement which began nearly two thousand years ago in a restricted area of the Middle East has actually gone into all the world. The penetration of the world by the Gospel of Christ is a direct result of the fact that Christianity is a missionary faith. If we are inclined to suppose that this is only natural, a little examination will suffice to make us realize that most religions of the world have never been imbued with the missionary spirit. We understand this better when we note that one important contemporary faith, that of Judaism, is not a missionary faith at all. Two others, Buddhism and Islam, are missionary-minded, but neither of these makes a serious effort to penetrate the entire world.

Even the humblest Christian is bound to be lifted when he recognizes that he is involved in a movement marked by genuine magnitude. In contrast to most religions, Christianity is neither local, tribal, nor ethnic, but is always potentially available to any human being, anywhere. At one period the followers of Christ were largely confined to the continent of Europe, but the day when that was true is long past. One of the striking sights at any world Christian conference is the degree to which every nationality is visible.

For the most part, the penetration into all cultures has been accomplished without the force of arms and without the employment of political techniques. There have been examples of forced conversions to Christianity, but it is important to realize that these are exceptions rather than the rule. The conversions which have been really effective are those which have come about by the convincement of minds. Though the spread of the faith has been unequal in different periods, and though it is far stronger in some places than it is in others, there is no area devoid of some reminder of the life, teachings, death, and resurrection of One who lived in Palestine nearly two thousand years ago. The Church has faced fearful odds in various generations, committed Christians usually operating as a minority, but the Church has both endured and expanded in a truly remarkable fashion. To try to tell the human story without reference to this is to create or to perpetuate a distortion.

It is common practice, in academic circles, to speak of "world religions," but it would be more accurate to speak of "religions of the world." In strict honesty there is only one world religion, the Christian faith being the only one which is worldwide in scope. That the universality is a recent development becomes obvious when we remind ourselves of earlier limitations. Christianity was once a faith chiefly limited to the white race, and only in the last few centuries has there been a radical enlargement, both in regard to geography and race. A century ago there was no Christian influence in Uganda, but now the Archbishop, who directs the work of the Church of Uganda from his headquarters at the Kampala Cathedral, is a black man. Only in the twentieth century has the major liberation from localism been accomplished, and the chief cause of this liberation has been the missionary movement.

The twentieth century has seen a notable increase in the numbers of missionaries operating in lands foreign to their own. At the present time there are in the world about eighty thousand such workers, divided almost equally between Protestants and Roman Catholics. While large numbers of the Protestant missionaries are supported and directed by denominational boards, several thousands of others work independently, arranging for their own financial support. Many of the Roman Catholic missionaries are members of orders which have come into being for specific missionary purposes. More than half of all of the Protestant missionaries of the world come from the United States of America.

Along with the striking increase in numbers in the twentieth century has gone an enlargement of conception of what the suitable missionary area is. It is now generally recognized that European countries and America are mission fields, as truly as are Rhodesia and Burma. There is, of course, an important difference in that the Gospel of Christ has been supposedly known for centuries in Western lands, but, as events have turned out, the spiritual need of the West is as great as that of any other area. The methods appropriate in the West may be different from those which are suitable in most of Asia and Africa, but the human need is no less great.

We get a better idea of the speed of the modern missionary movement when we realize that the most widely publicized of all missionary stories occurred only a century ago when Stanley and Livingstone met on November 10, 1871. The changes which have come in Africa during the single century since the historic meeting are truly revolutionary, and many of them are direct results of the very movement which seemed so feeble when Livingstone died on May 1, 1873.

The missionary story in the twentieth century has been paradoxical in that the period of the greatest growth has been simultaneous with that of mounting disfavor and criticism. One mark of current disfavor is the decline in the number of missionary volunteers in the colleges of America. A vivid illustration is provided by Mt. Holyoke, the oldest of the colleges established for women.[1] Earlier in the twentieth century, Mt. Holyoke was recognized as a prime producer of large numbers of missionaries who volunteered to serve both abroad and at home. Those who intended to engage in such work met together regularly for mutual encouragement and study in preparation for what seemed to them to be the noblest of callings. Today, by sharp contrast, there is no such organization on the Mt. Holyoke campus and no evidence of any interest in the subject. Some students speak of possible service in the Peace Corps or similar governmental agencies, but the careful listener hears nothing of a missionary vocation.

In the early decades of the twentieth century the Student Volunteer Movement was strong. Volunteer Bands were established in hundreds of institutions, but it is difficult to elicit the same response now.

The decline of student missionary interest in one sector has been balanced, surprisingly, by the emergence of new interest in another. While, on the one hand, it is not possible for the

1. The author was the Purington Lecturer at Mt. Holyoke in 1970.

Student Volunteer Movement to gather eight thousand students today as it did at Des Moines in January 1920, it is possible, on the other hand, to convene even larger numbers under different auspices. During the transition days from 1970 to 1971, more than eleven thousand persons, the largest student gathering of the kind in history, assembled in the facilities of the University of Illinois at Urbana. The topic was "World Evangelism: Why? How? Who?" This was the ninth in a series of triennial conventions sponsored by the Inter-Varsity Christian Fellowship of Canada and the United States. Every continent was represented among the speakers, and missionaries who attended reported that interest in overseas Christian service was as high as it had ever been.

The meeting at Urbana was undoubtedly a revelation. What it shows is that missionary interest depends primarily on conviction. Whereas it is obvious that the old kind of general student interest has waned so far as mission work is concerned, there is, in its place, a new interest based upon evangelical theology. The Inter-Varsity Christian Fellowship, being frankly evangelical in conviction, is able today to elicit a response which the conventional liberal stance cannot match. In short, missionary interest is by no means dead, but appears whenever certain conditions are met.[2]

Unequal as the Christian Mission has been in different centuries, all generations of Christians are bound to be inspired by the missionary emphasis of the first Christians. Starting with the supposition that they were virtually a sect of Judaism, the followers of Christ soon altered their vision radically.

2. It is an important truth, largely neglected by the current media, that the major contemporary Christian growth is that of evangelical groups. Read *Why Conservative Churches are Growing* by Dean M. Kelley (New York: Harper & Row, 1972). It will surprise many to learn that Kelley is a member of the staff of the National Council of Churches.

Much of the excitement which a thoughtful person feels in reading the New Testament arises from the unfolding of a revolutionary new pattern of religious expectation. Part of this change came from a careful examination of the Hebrew Scriptures in which the minds of the first Christians were steeped. While Judaism was not then, and has not been since that time, a missionary faith, there was within it a germ of the missionary idea in the teachings of the greatest of the Hebrew prophets. Early Christians were familiar with the conception expressed so eloquently by the prophet whom we call the Second Isaiah, especially in the words: "I the Lord have called thee in righteousness, and will hold thine hand, and will keep thee, and give thee for a covenant of the people, for a light of the Gentiles" (42:6, AV). The evidence that this prophetic conception was cherished and elaborated in the early Church is seen in the way in which the Apostle Paul made use, in his preaching, of the prophetic words: "I have set you to be a light for the Gentiles, that you may bring salvation to the uttermost parts of the earth" (Isaiah 49:6, Acts 13:47).[3]

The change which came by the maturing of the prophetic seed was so revolutionary that it cannot be contemplated without wonder. Though a background already existed, the change in practice amounted to a shift of 180 degrees. In spite of hints given by Christ Himself, it is obvious that at the very first His followers did not understand what was involved in becoming yoked with Him. Indeed, they demonstrated their profound misunderstanding by asking, near the end of His earthly appearance, "Lord, will you at this time restore the kingdom to Israel?" (Acts 1:6). His very last words on earth

3. Scripture quotations are from the Revised Standard Version, unless otherwise indicated.

constitute a clear rebuke to those who asked the wrong question. The task of His followers, He said with finality, was essentially centrifugal. Where, the disciples should have asked, are Christians to make their witness? The answer came as follows: "You shall be my witnesses in Jerusalem and in all Judea and Samaria and to the end of the earth" (Acts 1:8); "Go therefore and make disciples of all nations" (Matt. 28:19).

Indications of a radical new departure in religious experience were certainly involved in Christ's teaching, but only later could these be understood and appreciated. Now, with the advantage of hindsight, we can see how significant it is that Christ did not employ the concept of remnant, but used, instead, the utterly different idea of leaven. Superficially, the two ideas are similar, since both refer to what is small, but they lead in opposite directions. A people trying to be a remnant, keeping itself pure and undefiled in the midst of a wicked world, may reveal a certain nobility of character, but it is radically different from the pattern taught by Christ. The wonder of leaven is that it is effective, not by keeping itself separate from the world, but rather by *penetrating* the world. All that is involved in the Christian Mission was already present when Jesus said that the Kingdom of God "is like leaven which a woman took and hid in three measures of meal, till it was all leavened" (Luke 13:21). What had been implicit in the message of the greatest of the Hebrew prophets here became explicit.

The earliest disciples clearly supposed that they would stay in Jerusalem and associate themselves, in one way or another, with the worship at the temple. While the final words of the remarkable passage about the insight of Gamaliel reveal a certain greatness, they also reveal a self-imposed limitation of vision: "And every day in the temple and at home they did not cease teaching and preaching Jesus as the Christ" (Acts 5:42). Apparently, their original notion of a world task was limited by expectation that the peoples of the world would finally come to Jerusalem and be instructed there. Painfully, they saw the erroneous character of this expectation. The fall of Jerusalem in 70 A.D. verified the realization that the fulfillment of the prophetic dream would have to come, if it came at all, in a diametrically opposite fashion. This alternative way was that of diffusion rather than of ingathering. Consequently, Christianity has never, since that time, had a sacred city. Unlike Islam, Christians have no counterpart of Mecca and do not desire to have one. As the centuries unfold, Christians see increasingly the revolutionary significance of Christ's words to the woman at the well of Samaria: "The hour is coming when neither on this mountain nor in Jerusalem will you worship the Father" (John 4:21). A clear understanding of this dictum rings the death knell of all localism in religion. Christianity has many assets, but a geographical center is not one of them.

The earliest Christians soon understood that the Gospel had to be made known to all nations. All that they had to learn was the manner in which this should be accomplished, a manner which substituted the preposition "out" for the preposition "in." This matter of direction, which was crucial, had already been indicated by Christ, though they were unable to recognize it at the time, when He left the synagogue at Nazareth and sent His followers "out" (Mark 6:7). From that moment Christianity was a missionary movement. Indeed, Mission is really the oldest part of the faith.

The sense of direction outward from a center, rather than toward it, was fully articulated by Paul when he said that the

Gospel "is the power of God for salvation to every one who has faith, to the Jew first and also to the Greek" (Rom. 1:16). It took the powerful mind of Paul to clarify this directional change, enabling his fellow Christians to realize that they were "under obligation both to Greeks and to barbarians" (Rom. 1:14). It is in loyalty to this liberating idea that the Christian Mission has finally made Christianity the only universal religion.

Whenever essential Christianity has reappeared, often after periods of stagnation, the missionary aspect has been dominant. One vivid illustration of this phenomenon is provided by the outburst of vitality called Quakerism in the middle of the seventeenth century. Indeed, Quakerism was a missionary movement long before it was an organized religious body. Beginning in 1652 a remarkable band of men and women fanned out, usually in pairs, to any place on earth where they could enter. Spontaneously, and with very little prodding, their fellow Christians gave generously of their meager funds to support these missionaries in their travels. Many started out at once, following a creative fortnight with George Fox in the summer of 1652. By the end of 1653 at least thirty persons had gone out from Westmorland alone.

The expectation of imprisonment and other hardships, far from being a deterrent, seems to have spurred these missionaries on, as had been the experience among early Christians. Four were hanged for their faith on Boston Common, but this did not stop the missionary stream. The first Quakers, as they arose in England more than three hundred years ago, did not hope or expect to be anything other than Basic Christians, and, in the light of this expectation, they understood that Christianity is, by its very nature, diffusive. To ask, When did Quakers adopt a missionary program? is to state the question wrongly. As early as 1660 the words uttered on this subject were so clear that they are the rightful possession, not of one sect, but of Christians everywhere.

> For England is a family of prophets, which must spread over all the nations, as a garden of plants, and the places where the pearl is found must enrich all nations with the heavenly treasure, out of which shall the waters of life flow and water all the thirsty ground.

The modern chapter in the missionary enterprise has been marked both by a widespread enthusiasm on the part of lay Christians and by the formation of boards which have provided direction and support. In the twentieth century thousands of modest congregations, representing different denominational affiliations, have given regularly and generously to reach people in distant lands, though not one of them may ever be seen. I have witnessed, myself, the taking of a single offering for a medical mission in which the contribution of one congregation amounted to more than six thousand dollars. Some groups associated with what is called the Restoration Movement have had practically no central organization except that which is necessary for the collection of missionary funds. It is the Mission and only the Mission which keeps the individual churches of this order from being purely congregational. Among Southern Baptists the Mission is also the strongest uniting factor.

Modern missions, with their multiple features, have now existed for the greater part of two centuries. Early in the nineteenth century missionary societies and societies for the distribution of the Scriptures were springing up on every hand. The literary works of George Borrow give the contemporary reader some idea of the general excitement which the widespread distribution of the Scriptures provided one hundred fifty years ago, when even the children knew something of the magnitude of the various undertakings. In 1813 Macaulay, writing to his father from boarding school at the age of twelve, mirrored the general interest in the subject.

> My dear Papa,—as on Monday it will be out of my power to write, since the examination subjects are to be given out then, I write today instead to answer your kind and long letter. I am very much pleased that the nation seems to take such an interest in the introduction of Christianity in India.[4]

In the early enthusiasm for the World Mission many societies were short-lived. One of these, the Chinese Evangelization Society, was dissolved after a few years of existence, but meanwhile it performed an important service in that it sent to China, in 1853, James Hudson Taylor, who was only twenty-one years of age. When he went to China, Taylor learned the Chinese language and adopted Chinese dress as a means of identification with those whom he sought to reach. He returned to England, and in 1865 he founded the China Inland Mission which was, for a time, the largest single mission in the world. This great mission, which set the pattern for many others, was wholly undenominational and placed its primary emphasis upon evangelism. Evangelism and Mission thus came, for many, to be practically synonymous.

Though evangelism has continued to be important, the characteristic contemporary mission work includes many other aspects. Most missions now seek to penetrate the total life of a community, not merely in what has been known historically as evangelism, but also by means of a great variety of ap-

4. G. O. Trevelyan, *Life and Letters of Lord Macaulay* (New York, 1877), Vol. 1, p. 53.

proaches to human need. The most evident of these approaches are educational, industrial, agricultural, and medical, but there are now many supportive enterprises as well. For example, there are splendid facilities for radio transmission, one of the most professional radio stations of Africa being that established by Baptists in Nairobi. With the development of local publishing houses, much emphasis is placed upon the production and distribution of the printed word. Normally, wherever there is a well-established mission, one finds a hospital, an agricultural experiment station, and a school or schools. Sometimes this combination works with almost unbelievable speed.

One important part of mission work which was hardly expected in the beginning is its remarkable linguistic development. Wherever missionaries have gone it has been necessary for the visitors to learn the language, as Hudson Taylor learned Chinese. However difficult it may be for a Westerner to master the Chinese language, many others are far more forbidding because some have no written form at all. A language which is expressed in a literature is one thing, but the problem is utterly different when the language lacks not only a literature, but even the beginnings of a written form.

The contribution of the missionary movement to the understanding of languages, though insufficiently appreciated, is of immense value. The difficulty of producing a written form for a language in which not a single word is known is so great that the work is not likely to be accomplished at all except by a person animated by something as powerful as the missionary motive. Always the purpose has been to translate the Bible, because, if people can see or hear the Scriptures in the tongue which they already employ, a real start on evangelization can be made. At least part of the Bible has now been translated into about 1,400 different languages and dialects, and for the vast majority of the translations, missionaries have been responsible. Hundreds of languages now have a recognized grammar and a written form only because the Christian Mission has been the means of patient dedication, often on the part of men and women of modest powers.

Along with the laborious study of languages has gone the study of tribal customs, which has vastly enriched the science of ethnology. We know a great deal about primitive religions and tribal customs which could not have been known had the missionaries remained in their Western homes. Though it was not their primary intention to do so, several missionaries have turned themselves into first-rate scientists. One publication, which appeared in 1912, is *The Life of a South African Tribe* by Henri Alexandre Jarnod. This major work was made possible because the Swiss missionary lived and listened among the Bathonga people for thirty-two years. The dedicated missionary is in a strong position to understand a primitive people because, though he is an observer, he is more than an observer. He really cares about the people! The highest praise the local people often give to the missionaries is the sentence, "They have loved us."

One of the most revealing results of my effort to understand the phenomenon of the Christian Mission came as I sat with an African man and shared tea in his house. I noted that, though the floor was made of mixed earth and cow dung, which was well packed, the walls of the house were made of bricks. My host was enormously proud of his house, standing, as it does, in contrast to the rondavels of most of his East African neighbors. Because the house was made of brick and this was his chief source of pride, I asked him how he happened to have bricks available. "Oh," he said animatedly, "the missionaries taught us!" Then he brought out a faded photograph of the otherwise unknown emissary of Christ who had taught him to burn bricks. It was the same man who had taught him to read. I realized vividly how mistaken are those people who know of the evangelistic efforts of the missionaries, but know nothing else. The proud owner of the house produces better corn than is normally seen, as well as better coffee trees, and this he attributes to the influence of the agricultural mission. I realized suddenly, in an almost overwhelming fashion, that my host had experienced, in his own lifetime, one of the greatest enlargements that has ever been known in a short period, and that nearly all of it was possible because a few men and women had left their comfortable homes in order to work with unknown people ten thousand miles away.

The next day, after sleeping in the medical center of the mission, I watched as people assembled, immediately after the equatorial dawn, to seek help for their diseases. Someday the new state may be able to establish medical centers in sufficient number or quality to provide medical service for these needy people, but now, apart from the medical services which the missionaries provide, many people have no service at all.

It is important to recognize the degree to which the Christion Mission performs pioneering medical services. Very early it was realized that the Gospel, because it is total, must apply to the healing of broken bodies as well as broken spirits. After all, Christ spent much of His earthly career in ministering to the sick. Missionaries have now performed medical services for more than a hundred years, often instituting work which the government later takes over. Bishop Stephen Neill reports on this from his first-hand experience in India:

In one field after another, it was the missions which were the pioneers in service to the people. In the small part of South India which I know well the missions opened the first hospitals for women and children, the first schools for girls, the first asylums for lepers, the first schools for the blind and for the deaf. The government followed on long afterwards in all these fields.[5]

One of the most striking results of the Mission is that those who are affected by it quickly learn to give rather than merely to receive. Almost any heart is touched by the sight of produce being brought by people who have little or no money. They bring it to the rude church building as an act of sharing with those even more unfortunate and it thereby takes the place of a money offering in many localities. Furthermore, the new churches have begun to send their own representatives to open up new mission fields. They do this because, once they have caught the spirit of sharing, they realize that the one thing which they cannot do is to let the chain reaction stop with them. Seldom can they repay those who have made possible their own liberation, but this is not what is required. What is better is the giving to others so that the chain becomes longer.

There are, of course, numerous failures. When people are involved, it is only reasonable to expect that some recipients of help will be disappointing. Missions aid some people who turn out to be untrustworthy. Worst of all, rivalry and bickering among the Christian forces sometimes occur. In some places there are too many missionaries, all competing for the same people as potential converts. The greatest trouble comes not from the representatives of the big mission boards, who

5. *Call to Mission* (Philadelphia: Fortress Press, 1970), p. 8.

tend to allocate fields to one another, but from the individual missionaries who have dedication and very little else. Some of these have no people at home to whom they are responsible. The resulting competition is unfortunate, but so long as humans operate as a free society, there seems to be no way to avoid the difficulty. It is part of the price gladly paid for what is intrinsically great.

However inept some individual missionaries may have been and now are, the record of human service is so impressive that only a person of biased mind could fail to recognize it. Though the chief purpose of mission work is seldom that of social service, the mission almost always has a profound effect upon the social order and frequently helps to overcome injustice. The single example of the slave trade is, in itself, a matter of the very first importance, so far as human welfare is concerned. The evil of this trade was so terrible that it cannot, even at this late date, be contemplated without emotion. Many modern readers now understand the enormities of the slave trade better because of the brilliant prose of Alan Moorehead, especially in his book *The White Nile*. Only the truly hardened can fail to be moved by the following account:

> It was the women that the slavers chiefly wanted, and these were secured by placing a heavy forked pole known as a sheba on their shoulders. The head was locked in by a crossbar, the hands were tied to a pole in front, and the children were bound to their mothers by a chain passed around their necks. Everything the village contained would be looted—cattle, ivory, grain, even the crude jewelry that was cut off the dead victims—and then the whole cavalcade would be marched back to the river to await shipment to Khartoum. With the stolen cattle the trader would buy

ivory, and sometimes for ivory he would be willing to ransom a slave.[6]

The cruelty of the Arab trader was fantastic in its proportions, but he did not, of course, operate without helpers. While the trader was busy delivering his captives to the market, an African chieftain would often build up a fresh store of slaves, ready for the trader's return. In sharpest contrast to this was the position of the early missionaries and especially the most famous of them, Dr. David Livingstone. As a direct result of his faith, Livingstone, while not being naïve, exhibited on all occasions kindness, gentleness, and compassion for Africans. In this he was in marked contrast to some of his fellow explorers, and it was his missionary vocation that made the crucial difference. Consequently, he was, to his last breath, the avowed enemy of the iniquitous trade in human beings. Even before his death, this remarkable man dealt a blow to slavery from which it never recovered.[7]

It is wholly possible to have a religion without the missionary thrust. When this occurs, the religion goes on as a cultus chiefly directed to the welfare of its constituents or communicants. Without much difficulty, people can be satisfied with their own peace of mind or the cultivation of their own spirits. There can be emphasis upon worship or ceremony, with a priesthood and a valued ritual. In a real sense, people who participate in such religion tend to their own business and do not bother others. They can continue in this vein, devoid of mission, and maintain good relations even with an atheistic or dictatorial governmental regime. In the Soviet

6. New York: Harper & Row, 1960, p. 82.
7. Ibid., p. 106.

Union, for example, the government grants what it calls religious freedom, but only so long as people do not engage in missionary activity. There is no objection to religious celebration of marriages or funerals, and worship is neither supported or opposed, so long as it goes no further. A strong evangelistic effort, by contrast, would be opposed at once. Almost any government is willing to tolerate what it deems to be essentially harmless! This makes us realize how ambiguous the term "religious liberty" really is.

Though there is a profound sense in which, as the Archbishop of Canterbury has said, "the Church is by essence missionary," Christianity can continue for some time without recognition of this truth. One good illustration of endurance without mission is provided by the Amish. These people endure and even thrive in several American states, particularly in Pennsylvania, Ohio, and Indiana. They stay to themselves; they provide elementary education; they organize worship; they care for the religious instruction of their families. All this has about it a certain nobility which elicits a grudging admiration from their neighbors, but the striking feature of their life is their complete rejection of Mission. Since they are satisfied to leave other people alone, human beings who reside beyond their restricted borders are not their concern at all. The Amish, with all their hard work and reliability, have wholly missed the New Testament emphasis upon the necessity of becoming as leaven in the world. Instead, they provide the contemporary observer with one of the clearest examples of the contrasting conception of the role of the small group, that of remnant. If the purpose of religion is to encourage people to tend their own gardens and to keep themselves unspotted from the world, the Amish people are one of the finest examples of pure religion we know.

One instructive variant of the nonmissionary Christian experience is that of the once-flourishing Shaker communities.[8] In one sense, the Shakers were even more remnant-minded than are the contemporary Amish, because, unlike the Amish, they practiced celibacy without exception so long as they were members of the separated communities, those who decided to marry being encouraged to "return to the world." Producing no children of their own, these dedicated people depended upon conversions, which they strongly encouraged. Finally, early in this century, the number of conversions became too small to maintain the communities in sufficient strength. The Shakers were compassionate in that they served all who came among them, but they did not seek to penetrate the world except by the force of example. Believing that the world was due for imminent destruction, any widespread mission effort seemed to them to be a waste of time. Their hope, of course, lay in the expectation of the Second Coming. We should study the Shaker story far more carefully than has been done thus far, because, while the Shakers flourished, they came close to the exemplification of the Gospel, yet revealed a fatal flaw. They were right to reject the worldliness which they saw; the sorrow is that they could not envisage a different worldliness which is based, not upon separation, but upon penetration.

Whenever the chief emphasis is upon states of feeling, we are observing a nonmissionary religion. What is called emotivism today is vulnerable at this precise point. We can be glad for the stress upon first-hand religious experience, which was well represented early in the present century, particularly

8. The modern student can learn much about the Shaker experience of more than a century by visiting Shakertown village, about thirty miles south of Lexington, Ky.

in the wake of William James's Gifford Lectures, *The Varieties of Religious Experience*. But we can see now that this stress tended to leave out the missionary emphasis of Basic Christianity. Even in its very best periods, Catholic mysticism showed chiefly a concern for the sanctification of the individual, since mystics do not, for the most part, produce missions. There is, of course, something noble about any life wholly surrendered to God, or that is engaged in the attainment of private sainthood, but, in spite of this, there is always the lurking fallacy of subjectivism. The serious danger of all emphasis upon the inner life, if that is the end of the emphasis, is that of a high level self-centeredness. We are right to cringe when we hear people say that we must begin by loving ourselves. Though we cannot, of course, give what we do not have, if we start by thinking first of ourselves, we miss the point of Christ's teaching and draw a false conclusion from the Golden Rule. Christ's central paradox is that we must begin, not by loving ourselves, but by losing ourselves. Religious experience turns sour if it stands alone, and the man who worships only the God within ends by worshiping himself.

In the long run, the greatest harm to vital religion can come from the inside rather than from avowed enemies. The contemporary emotional wave represented by the renewal of the phenomenon of speaking in tongues may not, finally, be good news. While there is no doubt of the sincerity and the goodwill of those who encourage emotional expressions, they may actually be very far from the fullness of Christ. What they chiefly lack is the outgoing spirit. They miss the combination of service to the brethren and concern for the total welfare of people anywhere which the missionary movement has been able, in spite of mistakes, to demonstrate. Christians are always on the wrong track when they think the injunction is "feel," rather than "go." The hardheaded judgment of the Apostle Paul is the one which Christians need to heed today: "He who speaks in a tongue edifies himself" (I Cor. 14:4). The Apostle's central interest lies never, we must remember, in self-edification, however personally satisfying that may be, but in the word which "speaks to men for their upbuilding and encouragement and consolation" (I Cor. 14:3).

We can be grateful for every new interest in evangelism such as that evidenced, as has been mentioned, in the student conference at Urbana, but there is, in this, another subtle danger. Evangelism, without Mission, may become mere "soul-saving" in which the evangelist fails to involve himself in continuous humble service to those who have responded to his words. Though evangelism must always be a part of Mission, it is never adequate if it stands alone. Mission has about it an innate nobility because it provides the only known pattern in which the inner life of devotion can be combined with social action. Mission has intrinsic grandeur because it combines both worship and ministry, both evangelism and work.

Without the vocation of Mission, the Christian religion might continue for a long time, though in a fossilized fashion. There could still be the baptisms and the high holy days; there could still be some devotional reading; there could still be the cultivation of an intellectual system, supporting a highly prized orthodoxy in theology. Actually, some of the periods of greatest intellectual development have also been periods when the missionary movement has been virtually unknown. Orthodoxy was inadequate, not because it was untrue, but because, as Emil Brunner has shown us, it was purely defensive in its posture.[9]

9. *The Divine-Human Encounter* (Philadelphia: The Westminster Press, 1943), p. 39.

In an important sense, the case for the Christian Mission is really involved in the determination to demonstrate wholeness. A nonmissionary faith, however beautiful it may be in some aspects, is always a fragment of what is required. Because the temptation to fragmentation is constant, it is necessary in each generation to try to restate the vision of wholeness, but, apart from the idea of Mission, this cannot be done.

2

The Criticism of Mission

Charity begins at home.

SIR THOMAS BROWNE

Great as the phenomenon of the Christian Mission has been, particularly in the last two centuries, there is truth in the observation that it is now in abeyance. Both in reference to missions abroad and missions at home, there is an overcast, though overcast does not, of course, mean total eclipse. There are, as we have already seen, some evidences of vitality, and many other examples could be mentioned. The notable gathering of young people at Urbana must not be forgotten or neglected. On the home field it is significant that one of the most heartening of contemporary Christian stories, that of the Church of the Saviour, in Washington, D.C., is really a story of the resurgence of Mission. The entire membership of this vital congregation is divided into mission groups.[1]

The criticism of the mission idea is far more widespread than the literature would seem to indicate. Very few take the

1. See two books on the subject by Elizabeth O'Connor, *Call to Commitment* (New York: Harper & Row, 1963) and *Journey Inward, Journey Outward* (New York: Harper & Row, 1968).

trouble to write books in which their scorn of the mission movement is expressed, but this does not mean that the scorn is nonexistent. On a recent voyage by freighter I did not find one other passenger who shared my admiration for the characters of the missionaries around the world and for what they are doing. The low esteem in which the Mission is held is revealed in conversation, not so much by what is said as by complete avoidance of the subject. When the magnitude of the World Mission is remembered, we begin to sense the strangeness of such omission.

Something of the character of this cultural revolution is clarified for us when we read the works of John R. Mott. Much of what Dr. Mott wrote about the World Mission was inevitably autobiographical, since he was more personally involved in it than was any other single man of his time. In 1939 Dr. Mott published a book entitled *Five Decades and a Forward View*,[2] outlining the essentials of the missionary story in which he had performed a major role for fifty years. The five decades were the last one of the nineteenth century and the first four of the twentieth. The most exciting part of this story is that which depicts the "student missionary uprising" which reached a kind of climax in the third decade of our century. Now we are in the eighth decade, and it is obvious, in spite of a few exceptions, that much of the steam has gone out of the movement. Like Mott, we seek to have a "forward view," but we shall not experience recovery of vitality without effort, coupled with a clear understanding of the situation. It is important to try to understand the cultural forces which have brought what is at least a partial depression in the Christian Cause.

2. New York: Harper & Brothers.

There are still large nominal memberships in the churches of America and members still contribute many millions of dollars to the Christian Mission, both at home and abroad, but enthusiasm is clearly lacking. Most of the denominational boards are having trouble, as the eighth decade of the century develops, in raising as much money as was formerly contributed. This relative failure comes chiefly from a revolt of lay Christians who do not think that they are faithfully represented by the ecclesiastical bureaucracy. It appears, at the same time, that millions of busy men, who continue to contribute partly out of habit, have neither knowledge of, nor real interest in, what their denominational representatives are doing in foreign lands, considering this to be work which is rightly left to experts.

One mark of decline of interest is that mission study is often considered the responsibility of women and only of women. Though it is painful to admit it, Thomas J. Mullen is right when he says, "Both local and international missionary work in our parishes has been, by and large, relegated to the afternoon amusement of conscientious women, and the local church which cares very much about its denomination's program in Hong Kong or on main street is unusual."[3]

We understand better the magnitude of the task before us when we recognize that millions of alleged Christians do not visualize the Church as marked primarily by Mission. That this is true is indicated by the questions people normally ask. In overwhelming numbers the basic question is not, "What is required of me as a follower of Christ?" but, by sharp contrast, "What do I personally need?" In situation after situation, lukewarm attachment to the Church is defended by the

3. *The Ghetto of Indifference* (Nashville: Abingdon Press, 1966), p. 62.

remark, "I find I get along just as well without it," or "I am as good as the people who are involved." If we are seeking to understand, we shall pay close attention to remarks of this character, because each is a genuine revelation. The person who makes excuses of this kind has not begun to understand the idea that being a Christian means joining Christ's team and thus finding one's place in the total mission. What we must undertake, if we are to experience renewal, is not anything so simple as raising larger budgets for the foreign missionary enterprise. It must, instead, include the recognition by ordinary Christians that they are involved in an enterprise which includes not only giving, but also doing and thinking.

At this point in Christian history it is the thinking that must come first, for ideas have consequences, and it is chiefly by means of ideas that the enthusiasm for the World Christian Mission has waned. We dare not neglect these ideas in the hope that they will automatically disappear, for they will remain, and they will have even more consequences unless they can be answered. Hope lies in the fact that the pendulum has swung before and that it can swing again. It is in this connection that attention to history is truly heartening. In the history of Christianity not only dullness, but even fierce antagonism has been followed, in various centuries, by a revolutionary burst of new life. There is good reason to believe that the years just before us can, if the conditions are met, become some of the most exciting years in the entire course of the Christian faith. Fortunately, one of the conditions of renewal, that of self-criticism, has already been met.

Unless we are reminded of it, we may easily forget that criticism of missions has been experienced before and that it has been successfully answered. Indeed, some of the fiercest enemies of the idea of Mission have come from within the fold. Bishop Stephen Neill, himself an Anglican, has refreshed our memories about the kind of opposition which arose within the Church of England when modern forms of Mission were first seriously proposed:

> When the first missionary movement began in the Church of England rather more than a century ago, bitter scorn was poured on the idea of missions. Every attempt was made to prevent India from being opened to the Gospel. English bishops refused to ordain missionaries to go overseas, with the result that almost all of the first missionaries were German Lutherans and not English Anglicans.[4]

Opposition is therefore far from new. Even in 1932, when John R. Mott gave the Ayer Lectures at Colgate-Rochester Divinity School, he spoke of "the lack of sense of mission among so many men now holding positions of leadership."[5] What he observed then has grown visibly in the subsequent years.

We need at this time in Christian history to understand as clearly as is possible what the precise character of the opposing forces may be. It is especially important to take all questions seriously and to try to face the criticisms in their strongest forms. We dare not caricature the objections or minimize them if we mean to make a difference in the contemporary climate of opinion. The Christian operates best in the competing market of ideas if he maximizes the difficulties and frankly admits mistakes when mistakes have been made. The critics, we must remember, may have a point! We need all of the help that we can get, even from avowed enemies.

Some of the opposition to Mission naturally comes from the

4. *Christian Holiness* (New York: Harper & Row, 1960), p. 107.
5. *Liberating the Lay Forces of Christianity* (New York: The Macmillan Company, 1932), p. 90.

peoples of the countries where missionaries seek to serve. So strong is this opposition in certain areas that whole nations are now closed to missionary effort. In some countries, particularly modern India, those who are supported by mission boards are not allowed to enter and do work unless they have special skills, such as those of the physician or the agricultural expert. The one whose primary intention is to draw people to Christ is accordingly excluded. Some of this opposition is the direct result of rising nationalism, with its accompanying pride. Because admission that help is needed seems a shameful evidence of cultural weakness, articulate leaders condemn the Christian Mission as a form of imperialism. Missionaries are even accused of opening up new lands for industrial exploitation by the great commercial establishments, such as the oil companies.

However damaging opposition in foreign lands may be, the opposition in home lands, where the Gospel has long been known and where it has been partially effective, is far more damaging. Some of the opposition in the West is predictable in that it derives from avowed enemies of the Christian Cause. Some, of course, object automatically and predictably to the Christian Mission because they are opposed to Christianity itself. Among these, naturally, are both the old-line Communists and the New Left. The seriousness with which old-line Communists oppose the Christian Mission, either at home or abroad, is indicated by the fact that, in the Soviet Union, no religious instruction of any kind may be given to a person under the age of eighteen. This is another way of saying that when communism becomes really dominant, it denies the Mission to the young.

Opposition of this kind can be handled, but what is far harder to handle is the criticism of those who share some of the elements of the Christian faith and who do not, in most instances, really wish to destroy the Church. It is instructive that nearly all of the criticisms which stem from this general source are couched in highly ethical terms. While this is, in some ways, a reflection of the hypermoralistic and therefore unlaughing mood of our generation, it must be taken seriously, because it is seriously felt. The logic is curious, but the answer to that aspect can be given in due course. Meanwhile, it is important to observe that in every case the spread of the Christian Gospel is renounced because of adherence to some other and often partially allied gospel.

The first and in some ways the strongest criticism of the worldwide Christian Mission is a conclusion based on the recognition of our own failures. The history of ideas is the history of recurrent fashions, and it has become fashionable, in the latter half of our century, to malign ourselves. We may refer to this phenomenon as "cultural masochism." The speed with which people mount this particular bandwagon is amusing, but there is no doubt about the seriousness of the development, for, in all circles, it is popular to tell how bad we are. Why human imperfection has suddenly been discovered, no one takes the trouble to explain. We agonize over racial inequality, as though this were something novel; we suddenly learn that some people are poor. Where the people have been for whom this is such an enlightening discovery is hard to understand, but there is one thing that is abundantly clear: we are an angry generation! The hypermoralism naturally takes upon itself the task of finding scapegoats, much as the Nazi mentality focused on the allegedly evil influence of the German Jews. Instead of pointing to a race, however, we point to government and to business leaders, or, in some instances, to the Church.

The argument most often heard is to the effect that, when we have done so badly ourselves, we have no moral right to export our way of life. This criticism is based, in part, upon Christian principles. After all, we are taught by Christ to judge a tree by its fruits.

However sentimental the current masochism may be, our own imperfection must be freely admitted. Certainly the committed Christians will not deny it, since this is what they have been saying from the beginning. Long before it was fashionable to stress social evils, Christian spokesmen were emphasizing the sins of poverty, of racial injustice, and of militarism. Indeed, this has gone on for almost a full century in the promotion of what has been termed the social gospel.[6] We do not have the Kingdom of God on earth, and in the light of human nature, we are never likely to have it at any point in our earthly future. The critics, therefore, are on sound ground when they point to our own unworthiness. Furthermore, they have a particularly easy task. The critics of the Church always have an easy job, because the aspirations of the Gospel are naturally so high that they are never fully exemplified in practice. All Christians are vulnerable, because they honor a standard which they do not reach and by which they inevitably stand condemned. Every decent man is a hypocrite in the sense that his reach exceeds his grasp! But, of course, the critics of the Church may also be judged by the standards *they* fail to reach. Hypocrisy is no respecter of parties or of systems.

What we hear on all sides is that social reconstruction should begin at home. Let us, we are told, put our own house in order before we try to tell others how to live. Once we

6. The first Christian youth conference which I attended, in 1923, put emphasis on the very same evils now so generally deplored.

have all streams unpolluted, all races equal in opportunity, all education elevated to the highest possible level, all wars eliminated, all people with adequate financial support for a decent life, then, and only then, the argument proceeds, can we honorably seek to influence people of other lands.

Western civilization has, as everyone knows, numerous weaknesses and failures. It is in the heart of what historically has been known as Christendom that two world wars have been fought in a single century. It is the country which sends more workers overseas than does any other which experiences riots, the shooting of police, and streets which are unsafe in the darkness. These, moreover, are only a few of the evils of which we are rightly ashamed. The conclusion frequently drawn is to the effect that we have no moral right to make any item of our culture an article of export, thereby seeking to preach to others a gospel which we do not practice. While the observation of imperfection is beyond doubt, the inference is something else, and to this we must return in a later chapter. But it is important to mention at this point in the reasoning that, however valid the argument may be in reference to foreign missions, it has no bearing at all upon the idea of Mission at home, which may turn out to be the major Christian task for this generation.

The second major criticism of foreign missions, and sometimes of all forms of Mission, is inspired by the idea of absolute tolerance. Representatives of each culture, we are told, must be free to develop their own life-style, without the pressure of competing patterns. In one sense, this is an application of the Golden Rule. If I want others to leave me alone, I ought not to disturb them. If some people want to engage in polygamy, that is their business, and just because we prefer monogamy, we have no right to interfere. Each must have absolute freedom to go his own way and to express himself as he happens to like. Very few, of course, have examined carefully the logical consequences of this principle, but there is no doubt that great numbers now living in Western countries really believe that this is their creed and that they now apply it faithfully.

The combination of absolute freedom with tolerance of customs alien to our own is especially appealing in the field of religious belief and practice. The American experience of religious pluralism, though it has never been entirely satisfactory, seems to work reasonably well, and this is matched, in part, by the experience of various European countries and nations in the British Commonwealth. Nearly all nations, including Great Britain with its religious establishment, have accepted the principle of complete religious toleration. In spite of scenes of bitter tension and mutual recrimination, such as those recently occurring in Northern Ireland, most Roman Catholics and Protestants can live in the same areas with a minimum of conflict.

The general motto of mutual toleration is that of live and let live. If denominations want to undertake the added expense of maintaining parochial schools, that is their privilege. Every person, we love to say, must be free to practice his particular religion as his conscience may direct him, and those who claim to have no religion are equally free to proceed as they please. The First Amendment to the Constitution of the United States not only prohibits the establishment of any one religion, but also guarantees that each one who has a religion shall not be hindered in the "free exercise thereof." We know, of course, that this freedom is not so sweeping as it sounds. Those who, on religious grounds, believe in polygamy are not free, in the United States, to engage in it legally. Those whose religious convictions, if carried out to the full, would endanger the public health are likewise limited in the scope of their activity. Any religion which involves human sacrifice, as has been the case in many of the religions of the world, would not be condoned by any government today. While common sense, therefore, always recognizes that there are limits to freedom, the idea of toleration has won so much assent that it provides a generally satisfactory basis for living together in a multireligious society.

If mutual toleration is to be achieved, it seems to require noninterference. Many Jews, even though millions of them do not practice their own faith, resent deeply any effort at proselytizing by Christian groups.[7] In short, they resent missionary effort either of individuals or of institutions. But if the Jew is by common consent out of bounds so far as missionary effort is concerned, why should not the same pattern be applied to those who are sheer pagans and who desire to be undisturbed in their paganism? Carried to its logical limit, therefore, the principle of absolute toleration would prohibit all evangelism.

It is not hard to see that the principle of toleration, so often affirmed, includes religion in far-off lands as it includes faiths within the life of the West. If it is the duty of the Christian to leave the Jew undisturbed, why is it any different when the person involved is the Moslem in Egypt, the Hindu in India, or the Buddhist in Japan? If the moral law of noninterference in our own land is accepted, it is hard to see why it can honorably be denied in foreign countries. This seems, on the surface, to sound the death knell of the Christian Mis-

7. Some Christians join their Jewish neighbors in this conviction. The late Reinhold Niebuhr condemned Christian efforts to seek conversions among Jewish people.

sion. Practically every people and tribe in the whole world already *has* a religion. This is true, Dr. Schweitzer found, even of the supposedly backward people of West Africa where he served for so many years. Even though the religion of these people may not be so highly developed as is that of the Hindu, the same logic of noninterference would seem to apply to them as to anyone else.

A third criticism of the World Christian Mission which requires serious attention is that based on the doctrine of cultural relativism. This has some ideological connection with the principle of noninterference, but is different in that it goes much further. In its popular form, and sometimes in its academic form, this doctrine holds that, though cultures may be different from one another, they cannot be counted as better and worse. There is no objective standard, many believe, by which any culture may be judged. If, in some cultures, it is thought proper to wear clothing while in others it is thought proper to go naked, that is the end of the matter, for there is no extracultural court to which appeal can be made.

The chief intellectual support of this extremely widespread opinion consists of the denial of any objective reference in the realm of moral values. Thus, cultural relativism is, in reality, *ethical subjectivism*. It is popularly supposed that this position is the necessary consequence of the scientific study of sociology or of cultural anthropology, though, upon examination, the validity of the inference is far from self-evident.

That people differ about what they believe to be right is obvious and has long been recognized, since the orthodoxy of one tribe may be the heresy of another. Strict Hindus have concluded that it is immoral to kill a cow or even to eat meat, while people of the West often produce cows with the single purpose of killing and eating them. Since each group thinks its way is right, it is easy to see why some have concluded that there is no real right, and that differing moral standards are nothing but reflections of different cultural systems. If moral values are purely subjective, one value is exactly as good as another, since they exist merely in human minds and consequently have nothing to do with objective reality. Though, as we shall see in the next chapter, the case for the denial of ethical objectivity is not so strong as is popularly supposed, it is important that we face it without evasion. Unless it is understood, we shall not know why the enthusiasm for the World Mission has waned, and unless we have a rational answer, the future of the Mission is clearly in jeopardy.

Many of the overt attacks on the work of foreign missionaries are really variants of the cultural-relativity theme. Thus, we are told that the missionaries have bungled by making peoples feel that it is wrong for them to continue religious practices suited to their particular situations. A familiar example is the introduction of Western clothing among people who had survived for a long time without it. Have the missionaries, it is currently asked, really done any good? Perhaps the net result is a cultural uprooting which in the end does terrible harm.

It is in regard to religion that the argument of the cultural anthropologist appears to be especially persuasive. The religion of a tribe, we are told, is not a thing apart, but is intrinsic to the particular society, in which all of the factors affect one another. If the religion of a people is changed, or if the people are led to doubt its efficacy, the entire society may be consequently undermined. Because a whole people, when it loses the faith which sustains it, may actually wither and die, it is a serious matter to seek to change any man's religion, even though it be a primitive one. But the purpose of the Christian missionary, we must remember, is precisely that of producing such a change. Therefore, the argument concludes, the work of the missionary, however lofty the motives, is an evil one and ought, accordingly, to be opposed.

We get some idea of the change in the climate of opinion concerning the World Mission when we note that the word "proselytize" now has, almost universally, pejorative connotations. This was not always the case. Historically, the word "proselyte" merely denotes a person who has been converted from one religious system to another. Why this should be considered wrong is the important logical point. The only rational objection would rest, necessarily, upon a suppressed premise to the effect that one religion is as good (or as evil) as another. But once this assumption is brought out into the open, the thoughtful person is not likely to accept it uncritically. Indeed, as we shall see later, the falsity of the premise is one of the clearest elements in the entire discussion. Whatever may be said for tolerance, there is nothing to be said in rational terms for the idea of the equal worth of all religions. The notion that religion is intrinsically a good thing will not bear examination at all, for some religions, judged by their effect upon human lives, are radically evil.

Prior to an attempted answer to the popular criticisms of the mission idea, it is appropriate to recognize that the criticisms mentioned are more far-reaching than their exponents seem to realize. The arguments of noninterference and the denial of ethical objectivity do not bear merely upon work in foreign lands, but also upon work in our own land. If they are valid, they undermine what we try to do in Kokomo as truly as they undermine what we try to do in Kampala. Any mission which tries at all to reach the minds of people and to convince them of a set of ideas which they have not formerly accepted is indefensible if the familiar criticisms which we hear voiced are sound ones.

If it is wrong to try to reach the animist of West Africa with the message of Christ for fear of disrupting an existing pattern, why is it not wrong to try to reach the uncommitted resident of an American city who may be satisfied with his unbelief? If we are to be tolerant of everything, we shall, of course, have to be tolerant of the drug pusher who has found a way of life which appears to satisfy him. The same is true of the racist. Indeed, if we were to admit the validity of the major criticisms of Mission it would be necessary to denounce all of the efforts of those who call for immediate cessation of all preparations for war, for antiwar protests are meaningless unless they are efforts to change the minds of the people. It is highly possible that those who employ the doctrine of non-interference with the lives, the thoughts, and the religions of other peoples, are claiming more than they intend to claim. In any case, we cannot respect those who do not apply their own doctrine with thoroughness and with consistency. If the World Mission is wrong, then the Home Mission is wrong, too, for, in strict intellectual honesty, the adherent of non-interference can never undertake to evangelize anybody on any subject. He cannot, with consistency, oppose the Christian Mission, for then he is interfering with the missionaries! It is always intellectually dishonest for anyone to affirm a proposition unless he is also willing to accept all that the proposition implies.

Much of the widespread change regarding the World Christian Mission has come about by deliberate efforts to ridicule missionaries. As early as 1921 Somerset Maugham, in his story "Rain," influenced many minds in this direction by identifying the horrible villain of his tale as a missionary.

Maugham had no difficulty in presenting Mr. Davidson, a missionary to one of the Pacific Islands, as an inhuman monster. Davidson was shown to be crafty, cruel, judgmental, self-righteous, and, at last, in his reason for taking his own life, vulnerable. By clever writing, the prostitute was made to appear attractive, while the man who had risked his life in a medical mission was made to appear despicable.

All the familiar clichés about the effort to destroy local culture were, we must remember, trotted out by Maugham. The converts were forced to wear clothing which they did not desire; and happy music was forbidden on Sunday. "We had to make sins," Davidson told his companions, "out of what they thought were natural actions." "Rain" is really more than a short story; it is fundamentally a tract, in which supposed Puritanism is exposed. It belongs to the genre of protest.

Though the printed form had a wide influence, the subsequent motion pictures of "Rain" were far more influential. Whereas the critical reader might recognize that what the novelist provided was an obvious caricature, the vividness of the screen presentations made this kind of discrimination difficult and consequently rare. There is no way to know how many people lost their enthusiasm for the World Mission as a result, but the number was undoubtedly large. The experience of seeing the upholders of righteousness exposed is, of course, delightful, and it is especially delightful to those who are already moving in the general direction of permissiveness or the denial of an objective moral order. One important effect of the story is that it encourages the cultivation of the easy conscience. "I'm not so bad," the viewer says complacently. "At least I'm not so bad as the missionary."

In view of the existence of thousands of missionaries in the world, there may be, somewhere, a man as perverted as Davidson was. But to draw the conclusion that this is a true picture of missionaries is, by any reasonable standard, grotesquely unfair. Where one was harsh, thousands were and are compassionate, but when the exception is presented with such vividness, this is hard for people to remember. Any vocation could, of course, be pilloried in the same fashion. Though there are individual artists who are cruel, the caricature of these does not seem to bring the same pleasure that comes when an alleged ambassador of Christ is held up to scorn. *Elmer Gantry* brings pleasure to readers precisely because Gantry was a clergyman.

However damaging the presentation of "Rain" was in an earlier generation, the more recent motion picture "Hawaii" has been far more damaging. This picture necessarily included scenes from the early Christian Mission to Hawaii, because the Mission is integral to the modern cultural awakening in what is now the fiftieth state of the Union. Much that has occurred in the past century is the result of what the courageous New England missionaries once did. Though some reference is made to the courage of these men and women, who went around Cape Horn in sailing ships, the film, as it progresses, puts increasing emphasis upon one man whose unloving character is depicted in a variety of vivid details. The really terrible consequence is that it is commonly reported by viewers that at last they have seen an honest representation of missionary hypocrisy. Thousands have reached the completely unwarranted conclusion that the particular missionary was actually characteristic. Though it is obviously unintelligent to generalize in this fashion, the power of this particular medium, as it strikes the eye, is so great that otherwise thoughtful people do actually universalize from one instance.

"Hawaii," in cinematic medium, does not stand alone, but it probably constitutes the greatest single blow which the missionary idea has sustained in recent years. Part of what is involved is that great numbers of people are now provided with a largely unconscious bias against the whole conception. Perhaps they were oversold in the first place. Not all mission fields have been glamorous; not all missionaries have been good men; not all motives for participation have been un-mixed. People were given a romanticized picture of what the World Mission is, and now, as they move to the opposite extreme, the public accepts an equally distorted image. Dr. Visser 't Hooft, the first General Secretary of the World Council of Churches, recognized that popular literature has had a great deal to do with this. "The image of the missionary in the modern novel," he said, "is generally that of an incredibly narrow-minded person who has not the slightest under-standing of the people and culture to which he has been sent." So great is the impact of this one-sided view that the very word "missionary" brings to many contemporary people visions of ghosts from what they feel is a reactionary past.

The fact that relatively few have an adequate chance to correct their assumptions by the test of experience is unfortunate, but there seems little chance of altering this particular situation. Consequently, the hope of a recovery of fairness appears to lie largely in the encouragement of inquiry and the spirit of true criticism. As it has, in the past, been right to view the missionary movement critically, so now it is right to view the antimissionary movement with equal criticism.

Perhaps the opponents can be reached if they see that those who defend the World Mission are keenly aware of dangers and mistakes. It is worthwhile, in this connection, to recognize that denominationalism, whether at home or abroad, can become a hindrance to the total effort. Because, in honesty, we must admit that more money can be raised for the foreign task by working through denominational units, for denominational organizations no apology is required. Denominations are still manageable units of operation and do no real harm on the home front, but they may do incalculable harm in emerging countries. There is always a touch of absurdity about the exportation of affiliations which make sense in one country, but make none in the lands to which they are exported. There is something laughable about a Church of Scotland in Singapore. It is not required of us, in our forthright defense of the general Christian Mission, to try to defend what is patently indefensible.

The deepest danger of denominationalism, which appears in lands where the Gospel is a novelty, is not that of the perpetuation of old denominational loyalties, but rather the creation of new ones. In contemporary Africa there are now militant sects which are totally unknown in the West and which seem to proliferate as they divide. Some of these, unfortunately, present the Gospel in a diluted form, with a strong admixture of conscious paganism, particularly in ritual. This is one of many problems which, seen alone, might make people turn against the Mission, but there is nothing really new about such a development. Dangers are the price of anything of real worth, and the Christian Mission is no exception to this rule.

Possibly the greatest loss which has come in the present popular antagonism to the Christian Mission appears, not in the decline of financial contributions, but in the difficulty of securing high-level recruits for all kinds of mission work. Once, as we have already observed, it was reasonably easy to find missionary volunteers among the most gifted and intelligent of our young men and women. We could then choose among the best equipped. Now, however, the ablest tend to be drawn into other fields of work, and do not even give the missionary vocation a chance. Unless this changes, the prospect is far from bright, but a radical change can be effected if the truth is fairly presented. The criticisms must be met; the deepest reasons for Mission must be given; the climate of opinion must be altered.

In his monumental History of the Expansion of Christianity series, Professor Latourette refers to the period 1800-1914 as "The Great Century" and devotes three of his seven volumes to it. Much of the impressive expansion in those particular years was made possible by almost uncritical acceptance among the rank and file of the validity of mission. The conviction that Christianity must penetrate the world was accepted as self-evident by millions of Westerners without argument and without reservations. There were not many to doubt the dictum subsequently expressed by D. T. Niles when he said, "In order to be a Christian one has to partake in mission."[8]

Now all this is different and those who are committed to Mission need to know that it is different. If an answer cannot be given to the voluble critics, much, in addition to foreign missions, will be recognized ultimately as untenable. The best Christian thought of the last half of the twentieth century has been centered, in many instances, upon the application of the mission idea to the entire Christian Cause. This has indeed been the central conception in the movement widely heralded

8. *Upon the Earth* (New York: McGraw-Hill Book Co., 1962), p. 244.

as Church Renewal. Two of the most influential books on renewal illustrate this vividly, one of these employing the word "mission" even in its title. This is a book by Wallace Fisher, *From Tradition to Mission*.[9] Another book, *New Life in the Church*,[10] by Robert Raines, starts with "The Loss of Mission" and ends with "The Recovery of Mission." In this emphasis, many have seen the basis of new hope, but the hope is manifestly vain if the basic conception of Mission is unsound.

What is at stake, therefore, is far more than the financial support of some denominational mission board. In a deep sense, the entire Christian Cause is at stake. Unless there is real validity in the idea of Mission, Christians may as well accept with resignation the frequently repeated conclusion that we are finally living in the post-Christian Age. If this is a valid conclusion, it is helpful to find it out and bring a pathetic delusion to an end. If this is not a valid conclusion, we need to know why it is not valid and to understand the reasons so clearly that we can express them coherently to others. Only in this way can the pendulum swing again, and only by this means can support for an enterprise of intrinsic grandeur be renewed.

Hope of renewal of respect for the Mission is justified by isolated signs; the bones may seem to be dried, but they are far from lifeless. It is rational to believe that the miracle of renewal, which has occurred before, can occur again, but the popular criticism which is strong in some areas, though not in all, will grow in effectiveness if it is not answered in a reasonable fashion and answered soon. That is why the most im-

9. Nashville: Abingdon Press, 1965.
10. New York: Harper & Row, 1961.

portant crisis in the Christian Mission is not financial, but intellectual. Those who believe in the Mission have many tasks, but their first task is to think! If they do this, a true renaissance is possible, but if they do not, the erosion, which is already evident, will proceed unchecked until what has been a remarkable success may end in dismal failure.

3

The Defense of Mission

The only reason for being a Christian is the
overpowering conviction that the Christian
faith is true.

STEPHEN NEILL

The value of intellectual inquiry lies not in its ability to tell us what we ought to do, but rather in its ability to surmount the barriers that hinder our doing. The careful study of the philosophy of religion is helpful, not because in most instances it brings men to God, but because it fulfills the humbler role of removing barriers to requisite commitment. The first task, therefore, of those who believe that the case for the World Christian Mission is a valid one, is that of a direct answer to the criticisms of the Mission which are so commonly and so confidently made in our generation. Though each of the criticisms outlined in the preceding chapter is impressive when first presented, the impressiveness is lessened when we examine both the evidence and the logic.

The argument that our own failures should tie our hands sounds attractive, when we first hear it, because it seems to express genuine humility. Humility, however, though it is a virtue, is not the only virtue. There is also honesty and it is clearly dishonest to make imperfection an excuse for inaction in one realm when we do not practice consistency by applying it in others. We obviously try to extend the advantages of education as widely as possible, even when we are well aware that our schools and colleges are vulnerable to criticism at many points.

We have made a significant start on honest thinking when we recognize the profound danger of all perfectionism. Perfectionism is damaging to the human venture because it cuts the nerve of all effort. If I refuse to participate in an operation until I can approve every part of it, I shall wait forever. This is the meaning of the initially mystifying aphorism to the effect that the ideal best is the enemy of the concrete good! Unfortunately, it is our destiny to work in the middle and to try to improve what is less than ideal, the only practical alternative to this exasperating situation being that of doing nothing. Since the people who wait for Utopia necessarily wait forever, the intelligent question in every human predicament therefore becomes "What are the alternatives?"

The defender of the Christian Mission has no need to claim that all is lovely in the West; in like manner, he need not try to maintain that all is satisfactory in the Church, for whether at home or on the Mission field, the Church is always inadequate. The Church, we are forced to conclude, is of divine origin because, if it were only human, it could not have survived, but the truth is that it has survived through many centuries both the wrath of its enemies and the ineptitude of its members. At the same time the Church is human, and therefore fallible. A generation of Christian thinkers has been helped by the late Reinhold Niebuhr's emphasis upon the intrinsic imperfection of the Church and his consequent re-

jection of what he labeled "the great heresy of Roman Catholicism." This heresy, he said, is that of "identifying the
Church with the Kingdom of God and making unqualified
claims of divinity for this human, historical and relative institution."[1]

Once we admit that the Christian Movement, like any other
aspect of civilization, is vulnerable to criticism, we are free to
go on and to try to explain something which the critics often
miss, viz., that there is a real difference between Christianity
and Western culture. The claim that missions are mere door-
openers for colonialism and imperialism loses much of its persuasiveness when we observe the degree to which the Church
in missionary lands has been among the most active opponents
of imperialism. It is the conscious strategy of the Mission, in
a great many different countries, not to impose the culture of
the areas from which the workers happen to come, but to
develop local churches which are, insofar as is possible, indi-
genous to their own cultures. The contemporary missionaries
have actually gone so far in this direction that they have allowed those whom they serve to interpret much of the Biblical story in terms of their own culture. It impressed me to see
a church building in Rhodesia in which murals decorating the
exterior walls depicted well-known Biblical characters with
African features. The claim that the missionary attempts to
reproduce Middletown seems to be made chiefly by people
who have never had the opportunity to observe, at first hand,
the work which they criticize.

While the nineteenth century was the century of coloniali-
zation and imperialism, particularly in the splitting up of the
African continent by European powers, our own century has

1. *Beyond Tragedy* (New York: Charles Scribner's Sons, 1946), p. 121.

witnessed a reversal of this trend, and in this change the Christian Mission has had a conspicuous part. The practice of the missionary churches has provided a startling contrast to the once-accepted political procedure of the imposition of one nation's will upon another nation. Volume V of the influential Interseminary Series provided a clear answer to the charge of cultural imperialism in words worthy of repetition now:

> With due allowance for individual exceptions, it is true that the missionaries and their followers in the various lands were not, by and large, the tools of imperialism, whether cultural, economic, or political. They were carriers of the Gospel, for which claims conclusive evidence is found in the existence of native churches throughout the world, which are among the most vigorous critics of the general imperialism of the earlier day and the present.[2]

The critics who say that the missionaries ought not to transport Western customs into areas where they are unsuitable are often unaware of the degree to which makers of missionary policy have been insisting on this very point for many decades. The advice sent out from Rome from the Sacred Congregation for the Propagation of the Faith, as early as 1659, was clear and explicit on this point:

> Do not regard it as your task, and do not bring any pressure to bear on the peoples, to change their manners, customs, and uses, unless they are evidently contrary to religion and sound morals. What could be more absurd than to transport France, Spain, Italy, or some other European country to China? Do not introduce all that to them, but only the faith, which does not deprive or destroy the manners and customs of any people, always supposing that they

2. Robert S. Bilheimer, *What Must the Church Do?* (New York: Harper & Brothers, 1947), p. 42.

are not evil, but rather wishes to see them preserved un-
harmed. . . . Do not draw invidious contrasts between the
customs of the peoples and those of Europe; do your utmost
to adapt yourselves to them.

To the argument about absolute tolerance, as to that about
imperfection, it is helpful to bring the test of honesty. Those
who reject the Mission abroad on the ground of noninterference clearly do not practice this doctrine at home. Many
of those who criticize missions are themselves protest march-
ers and thus very far from consistency in their reason for
rejecting the missionary enterprise.

The idea that each culture should be permitted to proceed
on its own way, with no interference from the outside, is
really very far from a cogent one. It rests ultimately upon the
assumption that all cultures are equally good, each being best
for its own situation, but this is really nothing more than an
unsupported dogma. Some cultures ought to change! Whether
those living in warm climates should wear clothing or not may
be treated as a minor question, but whether women shall be
forced to do the backbreaking work while the men do no
physical labor is a question of a wholly different character.
To see a man place a heavy load upon his wife's back while
he walks on, totally unencumbered, is likely to help an im-
partial observer to overcome latent sentimentality about the
sacredness of local customs. Some liberation of women from
destructive toil is necessary if we are to have any approxima-
tion to the good life for all, and the truth is that this liberation
comes more rapidly through the impact of the Gospel than
it does in any other way which is known to us.

Perhaps there is no area in which the sentimentality of the
West is more grotesque than in our admiration for primitive
religions. One would suppose that after so many years of ex-

perience, the eighteenth-century fiction about the noble savage would have been totally extinguished, but apparently it has not been. The people who claim that we should never disturb a religion, or seek to provide a better one, are still suffering under a pathetic fallacy. No one in the twentieth century has helped more to bring realism into this religious discussion than has Dr. Albert Schweitzer. Though Dr. Schweitzer had great respect for the West Africans whom he served, he had no illusions whatever about the damaging effects of their religious ideas. Indeed, one of his major efforts was not merely to relieve their physical pain, but to liberate their minds.

When a child was born in the Lambarene hospital, it was the local practice for both the child and the mother to be painted white, all over face and body, so as to make them look terrifying. "The object," wrote the doctor, "is to either frighten or to deceive the evil spirits which on such occasion have a special opportunity of being dangerous."[3] What Dr. Schweitzer had learned in Europe, as he readied himself for his arduous work, did not fully prepare him for the shocking degree to which the primitive religion he was to encounter normally fills the human heart with dread. His neighbors, he soon realized, were unwilling to walk in the darkness, not because they were afraid of other human beings, but because they were afraid of the evil spirits which, according to their religious belief, lurked in the forest eager to harm travelers.

One of the greatest surprises that came to Dr. Schweitzer was the degree to which the presentation of the Gospel succeeded in liberating men and women from irrational fears. When the convert believes the Gospel of Christ he is really involved in Operation Liberation, reminiscent of Isaiah 61:1-2:

3. *On the Edge of the Primeval Forest* (London: A. & C. Black, Ltd., 1924), p. 156.

The Spirit of the Lord God is upon me,
because the Lord has anointed me
to bring good tidings to the afflicted;
   he has sent me to bind up the brokenhearted,
to proclaim liberty to the captives,
   and the opening of the prison to those who
      are bound;
to proclaim the year of the Lord's favor,
   and the day of vengeance of our God;
   to comfort all who mourn.

This was made vivid when, speaking of the convert, the missionary wrote: "Christianity is for him the light that shines amid the darkness of his fears; it assures him that he is not in the power of nature-spirits, ancestral spirits, or fetishes, and that no human being has any sinister power over another since the will of God really controls everything that goes on in the world."[4] We must remember that the doctor-philosopher was not concerned primarily with practices, some of which are innocuous, but rather with ideas. The main thing, he discovered, is to help the primitive man to "understand that nothing —no evil spirit—really exists behind his heathenism." To leave him to his fears would not be a virtuous tolerance, as so many critics of the Mission seem to suppose, but a mark of cruel unconcern.

It is right to emphasize Dr. Schweitzer when we are trying to evaluate the popular ideas which would, if adopted, undermine the idea of missions. His observations deserve respectful attention because he was, at the same time, a man of superb intellect and also one engaged in firsthand experience. What he reported was empirical rather than speculative. "For the work which the American missionaries began here and the

4. Ibid., p. 154.

French have continued," he wrote, "I feel a hearty admiration. It has produced among the natives human and Christian characters which would convince the most decided opponents of missions as to what the teaching of Jesus can do for primitive man."[5] He found that, far from the spread of the Gospel being harmful to primitive character, it built upon native good nature and enriched it. Dr. Schweitzer did not deny the good qualities of the primitive man, of whom he said that "with Christianity added to his good qualities wonderfully noble characters can result."[6] Perhaps the greatest boon which the Christian Mission brings to the African is that, in many instances, he is liberated from a tribal rite and introduced to a universal ethic.

The criticism which is based upon cultural relativity is the most confused of all contemporary attacks upon the missionary idea because the critic who reveals himself as being one who thinks that all positions are merely relative, inevitably falls into self-contradiction. If there is no objective moral order, and therefore no real right, then there is likewise no real wrong. How, then, can the critic claim that the promotion of foreign missions is wrong? All that he can say, in intellectual honesty, is that he does not like it, but that is too trivial to be worth repeating.

If there is any justification of our contemporary concern about the state of the nation and about the evils, such as those of war and poverty, which are almost universally attacked, it is only on the basis that objective right and wrong actually exist. No sensible person gets worked up over his own subjective preferences. It is not possible to justify the effort to overcome poverty except on the understanding that a kind of life

5. Ibid., p. 167.
6. Ibid., p. 157.

in which human beings are deprived of necessities is really and truly evil. But if this is the case when the problem is that of poverty, it is also true in religions. If a religion genuinely harms human beings it ought to be resisted, and that some religions are harmful there is no doubt. For example, the ideas of the sacredness of the cow can be shown to harm human beings, since, in the working out of this system, the cow cannot be hindered in eating the food which humans need, yet the flesh of the cow cannot be eaten. The rightness or wrongness of such a system, of course, is to be judged chiefly in terms of consequences.

It is easy to see the deep inconsistency of any position which denies a moral order and yet is judgmental toward others. It is not intellectually honest, for example, to hold, on the one hand, the philosophical position that ethical propositions have no objective reference and yet, on the other, condemn those who pollute the atmosphere. Consistency requires that we cannot have it both ways.

The more rational we are, the more we are concerned with the objectivity of truth. Unless there is objective truth, independent of whatever we happen to like, careful inquiry into anything is a meaningless undertaking. This is true in regard to the Christian faith and competing faiths. It is obvious that, though there may be elements of truth in all, the faiths cannot be equally true, because some assertions are in direct conflict with others.

Of course, we realize that we, in our finitude, cannot know anything perfectly, but that is very different from the conclusion that there is nothing to be known. It is essential to the major heritage in philosophy to conclude that although doubtfulness is intrinsic to our subjective predicament, such doubt does not deny the reality of an objective order, for any other position leads to utter confusion. We have good reason, then, to conclude that there is objective truth about everything—about atoms, about history, about God—our slowness in discovering the truth being irrelevant to it. Truth may be partly discovered, but is never made.

If we follow this tough-minded approach we shall appreciate the universality of truth. To say that God exists for one tribe but does not exist for another is simply to abuse language and to create consequent confusion. Once we make clear what we mean when we refer to God, we can be sure that He either *is* or *is not*. Either He is a Person or He is not a Person. To try to avoid this sharpness by saying that God is suprapersonal provides no logical escape, for whatever is suprapersonal is at least personal, though more. If Christ is trustworthy, then the individual who claims that God is impersonal is simply wrong. Alec Vidler has contributed to clarity at this central point of the discussion by saying, in reference to the Christian faith, "Either it is true for all men, whether they know it or not; or it is true for no one, not even for those people who are under the illusion that it is true."[7]

One of the clearest philosophical minds of our century is that of Paul Weiss, honored for his teaching at both Bryn Mawr and Yale. His contribution has been a frontal attack upon the behavioral account of man which "views all of his acts as equally valuable, important, ultimate, good, interesting." Such an account of man would destroy the missionary effort, anywhere, but this is not the special interest of Professor Weiss. His concern is to show both the limitations and the confusions which necessarily result if such a philosophy is claimed. He writes:

7. *Christian Belief* (London: S.C.M. Press, 1950), p. 10.

It has no right to say that one man had a better character than others; it cannot rightly condemn any act as
wrong or mistaken. Criticism, reform, punishment, remorse,
rewards, and education are for it arbitrary ways of making
men change their behavior from one mode to another no
less legitimate. A purely scientific theory which accepts all
human activity without prejudgment or evaluation cannot
cover all the facts. It has no place in its scheme for truth
or right. Yet it claims to be true and requires other views to
be false. Evidently it demands a dispensation for itself which
it cavalierly refuses to any other view.[8]

The rejection of missions on the basis of the cultural relativism which denies any objectivity to value judgments is
most vulnerable, from the point of view of common sense, in
that it denies the possibility of progress. If cultures are simply
different and not better or worse, there is no logical possibility
of progress whatever. The adherent of sheer relativism is
forced to conclude that the elimination of human slavery is
not an advance, since his philosophy has no place in it for such
a conception. All that he can say, in consistency, is that the
slave culture was one thing, while the liberation culture is another. But the plain man can see that a philosophy which leads
to such a manifest absurdity is itself absurd and does not,
therefore, constitute a genuine barrier to the missionary concept. The missionary frankly operates in the hope that progress can be made, and he is wise to hold to this, even when he
suffers many discouragements. In any case, he is closer to
common sense than are his critics. Because of our inevitable
finitude, we cannot know, beyond a shadow of a doubt, that
the philosophy on which the World Mission operates is absolutely right, but we can at least see that it has a manifest

8. *Man's Freedom* (New Haven: Yale University Press, 1950), p. 9.

self-consistency which stands in marked contrast to the self-contradiction of its critics.

Wherein does the validity of the Christian Mission rest? If it is dependent upon social service, it may be convincing for awhile, but it is not likely to be permanently so. Though missions can be honored for their far-flung work in the establishment of hospitals and schools, all of these may eventually be taken over and operated by governments. Indeed, much of this shift is already occurring in our own time. It is conceivable that someday governments will become sufficiently socialist to accept responsibility for every social need. It is even conceivable that a level of affluence can someday be achieved which will eliminate the necessity of caring for the poor. If, in the long future, these changes occur, the magnificent and compassionate social service performed in thousands of mission stations throughout the world will have historical interest but no more. Will the case for the existence of the World Christian Mission then be stripped of its validity? It will, unless there is another factor which involves real permanence. The conviction that there is such a factor has been the inspiration for this book.

The ultimate and permanent case for the Christian Mission rests directly upon the conception that the Christian faith is true. This is the one point which the critics of the enterprise do not touch, except by such an undermining of truth as undermines even their own criticism. In the long run, the best reason for dedication to the spread of the faith of Christ is the conviction that this faith conforms to reality as does no other alternative of which we are aware. Such a position is bound, in our age of supposed tolerance and religious pluralism, to be widely unpopular, but that is not a sufficient reason for rejecting it. It is required to find a *modus vivendi* according to which, while we seek to be tender with persons, we face resolutely all questions of truth and falsity, insofar as we are able to confront them. If Christianity is not true, there is certainly no adequate reason to reach people with its message, whether they live in China or in California. All of the service tasks can finally be handled in other ways, but the central message of Christ can be handled in only one way, i.e., by committed ambassadors. If the message is not true, the Mission will die and really ought to die; it cannot be maintained permanently by auxiliary enterprises.

There is, so far as we know, no individual in our generation who has made the question of truth so clear and so central as has Bishop Neill. Being a kind man, he naturally does not want to hurt those who do not accept the Christian faith. What do we say, asks this highly experienced missionary, when, as Christian emissaries, we are chided for our lack of tolerance? "We can only reply," he says, "that, whereas there should hardly be any limits to our tolerance of people as people, the moment we raise the question of truth, we are faced by the painful issue of the intolerance of truth."[9]

The phrase "the intolerance of truth" is one which deserves a wider circulation than it has received. However deplorable it may be, it is not possible to operate as thinking beings unless we accept the law of noncontradiction. However we may hate to face it, if one proposition is true, its contradictory is false, and if one is false, its contradictory is true. A vivid illustration of direct incompatibility is that of prayer. According to one faith, prayer can and does make a genuine difference in the course of events, rendering intercession for others a reasonable undertaking. By contrast there is a com-

---

9. *Call to Mission* (Philadelphia: Fortress Press, 1970), p. 9.

peting opinion which holds that prayer cannot make an objective difference, but it is limited, in its effects, to auto-suggestion. One of these is wrong!

There are not many persons who, when they really consider it, reject the principle of noncontradiction in the fields of science and of history. They would find it ridiculous to hold both that Julius Caesar crossed the Rubicon and that he did not cross it. If an astronomer asserts that a particular planet is devoid of atmosphere while another denies this, we may not know, with absolute certitude, which one is wrong, but we do not doubt, in the least, that *somebody* is wrong. Part of the current difficulty, however, is that numbers of persons who accept such realistic logic in reference to planets do not employ it when they engage in the study of religion. Here we seem to have something so intimate and so sacred that the ordinary principles of logic do not apply. It is probably at this point that the deepest misgivings about the missionary enterprise are felt, so far as ordinary decent persons are concerned. They hesitate to draw the practical conclusions which the intolerance of truth would seem to require. In this fashion, and without direct intent, well-meaning and compassionate people succeed in cutting the nerve of missionary effort.

We need to consider carefully what are the truth claims of the Gospel which are adequate to justify the immense expenditure of time, effort, and money which world evangelism requires. If it is a matter of truthtelling, the risk of cultural disturbance or even upheaval is worth taking. Though service to needy people is the practical object of the endeavor, the best service is usually accomplished by means of words. The conventional distinction between words and deeds, with the implication that deeds are valuable while words are not, is really a mark of confusion. It is by words, chiefly, that minds are enlightened and confidence restored. Of all ministries, none is more needed than the ministry of encouragement, which is carried on chiefly by the impartation of a message of some kind. This is, of course, a paradox, but its profundity grows upon us as we move into maturity. The Apostle Paul's statement of the paradox is "It pleased God through the folly of what we preach to save those who believe" (I Cor. 1:21). Those who lightly denigrate preaching will be well advised to think again. "By your words," said Christ, "you will be justified, and by your words you will be condemned" (Matt. 12:37).

The message which it seems foolish to preach, but which, in reality, changes thousands of lives, is the message of Jesus Christ. The missionary need not defend Western civilization or democracy or natural science or modern technology, though all of these include great merits as well as obvious dangers. He need not defend any ecclesiastical hierarchy or any particular form of church government, even though he recognizes that a person cannot be a Christian alone. The truth which the missionary proclaims, if he understands his vocation, is that God really is, and that He is like Christ. Being like Christ, the One who is Lord of all, including all nations, all races, and all cultures, cares for every individual and has made every human being in His own image. The consequent brotherhood stems from the divine paternity as it stems from nothing else in all the world. The effective Christian missionary anywhere is one who tells this story and tells it with all of the persuasiveness which he can muster. The Christian missionary is thus synonymous with a Christian, for one who is not a missionary is not a Christian at all.

The missionary movement, wherever it is effective, is consciously Christ-centered. The message is not concerned with speculation, but with what is held to be objectively true and with what has actually occurred. Insofar as we can assert any facts at all, we can assert with confidence that Christ really lived. His coming was a unique event, unmatched by any other event in all of history. He came to the best-prepared people on earth, at a time when the need was desperate and the opportunity for the spread of the message was greater than it had ever been before. In His earthly ministry Christ revealed the character of God and encouraged the love and service of men. He made tremendous claims, particularly the claim to represent the Father. This is attested, not only by the Fourth Gospel, but also by the Synoptic Gospels. It would be a callous reader who could fail to be impressed or even shocked by the words, "He who has seen me has seen the Father" (John 14:9).

After Christ uttered His most personal prayer beginning, "I thank thee Father, Lord of heaven and earth," He proceeded, according to both Matthew and Luke, to explain as follows: "All things have been delivered to me by my Father; and no one knows who the Son is except the Father, or who the Father is except the Son and any one to whom the Son chooses to reveal him" (Matt. 11:27, Luke 10:22). There is no passage in all of the Gospels which gives more evidence than this one does of being part of the original record which lies behind the completed books. Christ's words thus put before the thoughtful person an agonizing dilemma. Either He was telling the truth or He was an impostor or a madman. What is wholly indefensible is the posture of the person who accepts Christ as a trustworthy teacher, but deliberately neglects Christ's teaching about Himself and His special relationship to the Father. Those who reject Christ's extraordinary claims are forced into the uncomfortable position of concluding that He was either the great deceiver or the greatly deceived. Christians are convinced that He was neither.

The chief literary asset which the Christian missionary possesses in any land or in any culture is the New Testament. The recognition of this is what has led to the heroic efforts at translation in many obscure and hitherto unwritten languages. The people who confront Christ in the New Testament are introduced to an amazing story. They learn there that Christ not only lived and taught and healed, building up a small fellowship destined to continue against odds, but that He was crucified as a criminal and, after three days, rose from the dead. Is this true or false? It has to be one or the other, since we are dealing with statements about events. If it is false, we ought to forget it and get on with the task of making an imperfect world relatively better during the short time that is available. If it is true, we ought to share the truth as widely as possible, because it tells us something of transscendent importance about the world of which we are a part. It tells us, among other things, that ours is an open rather than a closed universe. It tells us that with God, all things are possible, thus emancipating us from the confining effect of naturalistic dogma.

An important feature of the story which the missionary anywhere has to tell is that Christ, having arisen, is alive today and can be known by anyone who will open his heart to His presence. The Risen Christ, the Christian believes, is available today, at any geographical point, and is actually knocking at every human door (Rev. 3:20). He, therefore, is more than historical though He is that; He is our contemporary Teacher and Encourager. That Christ is temporally available makes Him universal; consequently, the missionary is presenting a potentially universal faith. He is not the exponent of an American religion, for Christ did not come to America in the flesh. No new convert need be humiliated by the fear that he has adopted an alien faith.

The only real defense which the Christian Mission requires is the evidence that the story which it tells is true. Truth is not easy to come by in this world and certainly is not validated by mere affirmation, because human beings, in their fallibility, are exceedingly prone to error. Indeed, error is something of which we are absolutely sure, since there are contradictory claims and we know, thereby, that some claims are bound to be erroneous. If any claims are erroneous, it is a good thing to discover that they are, so that they can be discarded.

Because the stakes are so high, the Christian has a deeper incentive than anyone else to engage in what may be rightly called holy skepticism. To believe easily, and with insufficient evidence, is to be disloyal to Christ who taught His followers to love God with all their *minds*.

In trying to find out what is true and what is false in this world, we depend ultimately upon experience. In a profound sense, every man is both an empiricist and a rationalist, because all that we can depend upon is experience, plus a reasonable interpretation of it. The best evidence of truth is that in which we entertain a hypothesis which unites a variety of experiences, both of ourselves and of other persons, in the most coherent fashion. Unfortunately, we are never able to get behind experience to that to which experience points.

Even what is termed revelation is merely another kind of experience, namely, the experiences of direct confrontation with the Living God. The Hebrew definition of a prophet was one who had experiences of this kind.

Religious experience stands in exactly the same logical situation as does experience of a sensory character or any other. Of course, some may deny the validity of such experience on the ground that it is impossible, but inasmuch as this amounts to no more than the utterance of a dogma, it does not merit serious attention. Since we cannot proceed beyond experience, the rational process is to try to discover order *within* the experiences until we find real coherence. We do not, accordingly, have any absolute test of veracity anywhere, certainty being denied all who are in the finite predicament, but we find that some positions are relatively more convincing than others. If we must wait for perfection of proof we shall wait forever, but, fortunately, this is not required because we can have a sufficient measure of veracity to make life bearable.

Many people seem to suppose that there is some absolute test of veracity in ordinary sense experience, but reflection shows that none exists. I see an object and the question may arise whether this is just a figment of my imagination or is really there. I go over and touch it, provided the object is near at hand, but this does not take me beyond my original limitations; it merely gives me one more item of experience which strengthens the conviction because the different experiences are consistent with one another. Therefore, the only approach to objective proof which is humanly possible is necessarily that which is cumulative. In this connection, the enduring Christian fellowship is a fellowship of verification, as the experiences of one generation support those of another.

While all experience is necessarily subjective, it can point, in combination, to that which is objectively real.

Though the Christian is a believer, he is not a *mere* believer; he has a reason for the hope that is in him. The good news of the resurrection of Christ, for example, is supported by excellent historical evidence. The primary evidence is not that the disciples *believed* that He arose, but that, as the Risen Christ met them, they experienced changed lives. Once they had been broken and defeated men, but soon afterward they exhibited a courage and confidence which lasted, not merely for the moment, but for the remainder of their lives. They were immovable in spite of persecution and every external discouragement. How is the thoughtful observer to react to this kind of evidence? To speak of mass delusion is to reveal amateurishness, for this is not how delusion works. The changed men themselves accounted for the radical alteration in their behavior and character by the conviction that Christ had really risen, and that He had actually confronted them. It is important to know that the Christian does not believe in the Risen Christ simply because he wants to believe; he believes because the historical evidence points in that direction.

There is no way in which we can exaggerate the supporting evidence of the central conviction that what Christ taught is true and that His continuing presence is a reality. He appears to some people in solitude, but more commonly He appears to men and women in the fellowship. Imperfect as the Church is, and has always been, the central verifying experience is that "where two or three are gathered in my name, there am I in the midst of them" (Matt. 18:20). It was verifying experiences of this kind which supported the martyr, Dietrich Bonhoeffer, in his lonely ordeal of suffering and death. "There is probably no Christian," he wrote, "to whom God has not

given the uplifting *experience* of genuine Christian community, at least once in his life."[10]

We begin to have some understanding of the wonder of
coherence in Christian experience when we recognize the
extent of the verification. When He first mentioned the
Church, Christ said that "the powers of death shall not prevail
against it" (Matt. 16:18). All subsequent history has served
to verify this prediction. The more we think of it the more
we are impressed with the evidential value of the endurance
of the Church, in spite of attacks both outside and inside. The
miracle of survival is therefore not an empty phrase. Survival
does not, of itself, provide adequate evidence of objective
truth, but it contributes mightily to the totality of evidence.

The logical approach to the question of truth puts the
Christian missionary enterprise in a very strong position. The
missionary is thereby saved, simultaneously, from unnecessary
fixation of dogma and from the confusion of those who have
no firm place to stand. Far from being dogmatic, there are
numerous problems about which such an emissary is frankly
and deeply perplexed. His creed is not a long one, but, fortunately, it is not necessary that it should be so. The Christian
missionary believes one thing, and this one thing is of such
transcendent importance that it finally carries him as far as he
needs to go. He has only one commitment and that is to
Christ. Believing that Christ is trustworthy, he allows the
argument to go on from there, wherever the implications of
the central position may lead him. One of the most notable of
missionaries, George Fox (1624-1690), is reported to have
said, "I took men to Jesus Christ and left them there."

What is the missionary's right relation to those who have

10. *Life Together* (New York: Harper & Row, 1954), p. 39.

not yet been led to accept Christ as the Center of Certitude? He will have to avoid two contrasting errors, the error of permissiveness and the error of denunciation. The remaining road is admittedly narrow, and the gutters on both sides are wide, but this is the road which Christians are called to travel. On the one hand, we get nowhere at all if we repeat sentimentally the cliché about all roads pointing equally to the top. There is, as Scripture affirms, only one way by which men may be brought to the Father (John 14:6), and if we abandon this, we have little ground left on which to stand. In the refusal to abandon this particularity we have the encouraging support of many of the greatest minds, not only in the long past, but in our own century. In the brilliant Gifford Lectures which John Baillie wrote, but did not live to deliver, the author inserted, in this highly rational text, his own unswerving conviction concerning the position which cannot be abandoned. "I had of course," he wrote, "always believed that there is no ultimate salvation for mankind save in Jesus Christ."[11]

But what about the people who have not explicitly accepted Christ in this life? Are we bound to claim that there is no hope for them? By no means. For one thing, we are not the ones to judge, but, more importantly, we dare not limit God's power. It is undoubtedly true that Christ has been able to reach men and that He continues to reach them, even when they have never heard His name. Early Christians took care of this problem by means of the Logos doctrine, refusing to limit the power of Christ by their own conceptions. He can find men who, at least for awhile, do not know that they are found. Because Christ's light can reach every man (John

11. *The Sense of the Presence of God* (New York: Charles Scribner's Sons, 1962), p. 255.

1:9), the power of God to draw men to the one true Way is limitless.

It is not the missionary's task to pronounce all other religions and philosophies totally false, for they are not. There are great truths pronounced by nontheistic humanists, as there are valuable insights taught by Buddhists. In humility, the Christian must accept truth wherever it is to be found. What the Christian maintains, however, and what he is able to defend with cogency, is the conviction that whatever is true in all religion is genuinely consummated in Christ. "I am not come to destroy," He said, "but to fulfil" (Matt. 5:17, A.V.). About these words there is an amazing finality.

There is, we conclude, abundant reason to believe that the central convictions of Christianity are true and that the central commitment is justified. What follows then? Simply this: the saving truth must be brought to as many people as possible, regardless of where they live. The case for *foreign* missions, as against work at home, is simply the observation that geographical limitations do not count at all. Differences of geography and differences of culture are not excuses for failure to spread what men and women everywhere deeply need. Herein lies the cogency of the Great Commission.

4

The Field of Mission

The World is my parish.

The missionary program of the Church of Christ is not simply one aspect of the Christian Cause. It is, instead, the concept which is capable of bringing order and meaning into the entire Christian enterprise. The missionary idea becomes powerful to the extent that it becomes universal in the recognition that the vocation of missionary is really identical with the Christian vocation itself. Because a missionary is defined as one who is "sent," there is a strong tendency to think of the word as denoting only a small number who are officially appointed and consequently supported by their fellow Christians. If, however, we understand that Christ is the Sender, we have a means of overcoming this unfortunate fragmentation. We are then prepared to enunciate and to implement the revolutionary idea of the "Universal Apostolate." When they are loyal to the basic conception, Christians do not merely *send* missionaries; they *are* missionaries. The noblest conception of the true Church is that of a band of people who are engaged in ordinary life and who are conscious of their missionary vocation. The Church, in essence, is a missionary society!

Everyone who reads these words will realize, of course, that the churches which he knows do not fully demonstrate this pattern. Indeed, to some who call themselves members, the idea will seem unrealistic or even bizarre. In actual practice we are so far from demonstrating this pattern that the idea of the Universal Apostolate is not even considered, in many instances, to be a live option. In actuality we think that we are doing very well if we collect a few thousand dollars in one congregation and send it to a national mission board to be administered. No Christian will despise even this kind of giving, because impersonal as it necessarily becomes, it supports far-flung efforts which otherwise could not be continued. But, helpful as such support may be, it is important that we should never permit it to provide us with easy consciences.

However unrealized the idea of a missionary vocation for all committed Christians may be, the promulgation of this dream is far from a wasted effort. In all fields it is valuable to hold aloft ideas of genuine magnitude because, even though they do not achieve full embodiment, the presentation of the standard keeps us dissatisfied and prods us forward at least part way to the goal. This is why we can truly say that the standard is our most precious possession. While we do not, of course, achieve the standard, without it our spiritual poverty would be far worse than it is. Some people speak scornfully of the words "with liberty and justice for all," which Americans repeat in the salute to the flag, because these noble conceptions are never fully achieved. Of course they are not, for we are dealing with human ineptitude and greed, but it does not follow from the fact of partial failure that the ideal should not be reaffirmed.

The Universal Apostolate of mothers and doctors and farmers and businessmen has an inherent attractiveness. It is possible that our time may become one of the flowering periods of the Christian Cause, but whether it will or not depends in large measure on the acceptance of the Idea of Mission as both universal and regulative. If this is seriously attempted, it can revolutionize the entire undertaking. Herein lies the hope of a new Reformation!

The Mission of the Church is by the committed to the uncommitted, wherever they may be. This is the chief reason why mere Sunday religion will not suffice. Part of the contemporary stirring in Christian circles today is recognition of the need of going to people where they are. Why should not the Gospel relate to the communities where men and women work, and not merely to those where they sleep?

It is extremely fortunate for the Christian Cause that it is not necessary to try to get its missionaries into the world, since that is where they already are. Christ's ambassadors are already in the Teamsters Union and in the House of Representatives and on the automobile production line. The placing of potential Christian missionaries is so fortunate that it is almost fantastic. If the Church were limited to a shrinking number of professionals, there might be reason for discouragement, but there is immense hope in the scattering of committed Christians as they pursue their secular occupations. The practical task is to make them see the potential of their vocation and to try to help them to be prepared to fulfill it.

More and more the World Mission is now being described in other than geographical or even historical terms. It is not satisfactory to speak of missions as "foreign" and "home," and there is a subtle snobbery in referring to "older" and "younger" churches. By contrast, new and meaningful classifications of the total Mission may profitably be stated in terms of employment. There can be one kind of effort in industry, another in the universities, another in government, and so forth. In the striking phrase of Matthew 13:38, "the field is the world," but, in practice, each person must find his own way in which to participate in the total field.

Because industry is important for contemporary civilization not only in developed, but also in partially undeveloped countries, thoughtful Christians must concentrate much of their attention upon the Industrial Mission. The Industrial Mission is in some ways a frustration as well as a promise. Everyone knows that something ought to be done, but no one claims to know exactly the way to begin. It is possible to handle the work of a local parish reasonably well because of the advantage of an accepted pattern of action and its consequent momentum. Thus a local church may sometimes keep going for a long time, in spite of unimaginative leadership. But for Christian work in the refrigerator factory there is no accepted pattern, and, with all the goodwill in the world, we do not know what to do. No group of Christians dare claim it has succeeded in this important field. Local pastors take turns going to factories on particular days, but they are puzzled about how to proceed. They wonder, honestly, if the system is really touched in any significant fashion.

It may not be a complete answer, but we have at least made a start when we recognize that the main components of factories are persons and that the normal person is needy. He needs someone who will listen patiently as he presents his problems and he needs someone who will care. It is a true beginning of Industrial Mission, not merely when professionals enter the working scene, but when Christian workers look upon their fellow workers as their field and try to provide both listening and caring. The major function of the professionals should be the training of workers in order that they may be equipped to perform this ministry as no outsider can.

One of the most experienced of all who are concerned with the Mission to Industry is William Gowland, of Luton, England. On the basis of experimentation in many factories, Gowland concludes that there is no chance of real effectiveness merely in the employment of chaplains who carry on pastoral work in industrial plants. It is his observation that "we must frankly recognize the infiltration of the Gospel into industry as essentially the task of the laity, and it must be done with a conscious sense of mission on their part. A factory chaplain can do a lot, but when contrasted with the opportunity presented to them it is really very little."[1]

The best missionary work in scenes of employment is not likely to be accomplished by "worker-priests," for these men are quickly spotted and their influence is limited by the fact that they are looked upon as professionals. Rather, it is likely to be done by missionaries who preserve their lay status and thus relate, on the basis of equality, to their fellow workers.

The degree to which ordinary people want listeners can hardly be exaggerated. The head of a department reports that her main function is not, as she supposed, to deal with problems of administration, but rather with personal problems. Some large corporations employ professional counselors for this purpose. One committed Christian who is the president of a factory actually talks with more workers about personal difficulties than about difficulties of production and distribu-

1. *Militant and Triumphant* (Nashville: Tidings, 1953), p. 37.

tion. This is the way it ought to be. People need pastors, and the sad truth is that the majority of people in the modern world have none. The employee makes an appointment ostensibly because of professional reasons, but actually because of problems of family, of the right selection of a new chapter in life, or of the discovery of a way in which faith can be maintained with intellectual integrity.

Far from the missionary enterprise becoming obsolete, it now has new potential significance. We must see new areas as mission fields. One of the most obvious of these is the university campus where we have a really new situation. Historically, at least in America, there has been an intimate connection between the Christian faith and higher education. For decades, nearly all of the colleges which were established were founded by Christian concern and sacrifice, but today this bond is largely severed. All about us are institutions which, in honesty, must be described as "ex-Christian colleges." These may now rightly be looked upon as mission fields, and fields of enormous difficulty. Anyone who speaks in a variety of educational institutions normally reports that it is harder for the avowed Christian to secure a fair hearing in a college which was once unapologetically Christian, but is so no more, than it is in one which is frankly secular.

The missionary to academia often faces greater odds than does the missionary to Kenya. Bishop Neill, who now serves in Kenya, but who knows the American campus well, attests to this judgment. "On every American campus," he says, "the student is assailed by a myriad of voices, assuring him that the Christian faith belongs to an outworn age and that the churches have fatally betrayed their trust."[2] In the standard

2. *Call to Mission*, op. cit., p. 88.

academic situation today there is neither freedom nor equality of opportunity, so far as the market of ideas is concerned. Because nothing is worse than the complacency of false optimism, the would-be academic missionary needs to face the gravity of his struggle. In some universities the opposition includes the paid employees of the churches who manage student "foundations" but are, in many instances, satisfied to engage in social action and do not even claim to have a committed faith to impart. It is not only in the University of Moscow that there is uncritical acceptance of the doctrine that science has made a religious faith obsolete; this same position is promoted, without examination, in many universities of what we are pleased to call the free world.

As in the world of industry, so in the academic sphere it is likely that the best hope of penetration will come, not by the introduction of outsiders, but by those who are already involved. There is real hope in the formation of guilds of Christian intellectuals within the various faculties. Great changes may come through the influence of small bands of scholars who may be competent in science or literature or law and who, at the same time, are unashamedly committed to Christ. Their first task is to engage, not singly but together, in the support of a theistic world view in the face of a naturalistic establishment. Alone, the Christian scholar may be tolerantly neglected, but a genuine, well-knit group can work wonders. Such a group can, if it means business, be formed on the campus of every American college. As Student Volunteer Bands devoted to work abroad were once formed, it may now be wise to form Faculty Volunteer Bands which will be prepared to help one another in the penetration of the particular mission field where they live.

Bleak as the prospect for the academic mission appears to

be, a little attention to history will suffice to indicate that the situation is not hopeless. Because radical changes have taken place before, it is not unreasonable to suppose that they can take place again. There are few chapters in the history of higher education more encouraging than that of the presidency of the great Timothy Dwight at Yale, which began in September 1795, and which marked a new era in the life of the college. We are indebted to Charles E. Cuningham for his brilliant biography of the famous president, which includes a detailed and dramatic account of how, under Dwight's leadership, the entire mood of the institution changed, so far as Christian commitment was concerned. Cuningham has helped his readers to understand something of the truth of Lightfoot's aphorism that "the study of history is a cordial for drooping spirits."

When Dwight became president of Yale, the anti-Christian forces were so solidly in control that a reversal of the situation seemed hopeless. The new class that entered in the autumn of 1796 included only one freshman who was a "professing Christian," while the sophomore class contained none. "One Communion Sabbath," records Cuningham, "impious scoffers in the dining hall cut the bread in pieces, and with unctuous mockery offered the elements to a solitary student who had just come from the table of his Lord."[3] The college church had itself dwindled to two members.

Dwight's strategy was to force the enemy to take the defensive. He encouraged the students to debate openly the validity of the Christian faith, allowing each student to state his case without fear of reprisal, and then the president entered the lists himself. "Shunning battle was not Dwight's way of

3. *Timothy Dwight: A Biography* (New York: The Macmillan Company, 1942), p. 302.

winning a war. He struck in the open, full and hard, where all the world could see the foe fall. Almost before the campaign had opened, this decisive victory at the outset started the rout of infidelity."[4] For the next six months President Dwight preached steadily on the central subject. Though his eyesight became so bad that only with the greatest difficulty could he write or read a single sentence, he still preached twice every Sunday, taught his class, and administered the college. He added to his official duties a special set of lectures on Evidences of Divine Revelation. Thus, "he drove infidelity from first one lurking place then another."

After long and patient waiting, in the spring of 1802, a momentous religious revival occurred. Providence, at last, saw fit to reward a faithful servant's labors by sending down a shower of grace. One third of Yale's two hundred and thirty students became hopefully converted. Over thirty of these entered the ministry, while the others, in various ways throughout their lives, spread its influence.[5]

Some externals of living have changed since Dwight's day, and our academic mission fields are more complex than was his, but details do not alter the major challenge. What has been done before can again be done, provided Christians employ their intellectual resources. Because defenders of the faith have been able to outthink opposition so many times in the past, there is no reason to conclude that they must retire in defeat at this particular date. Human need has not changed and God's truth is not altered by passing fashions.

One of the reasons why so many Christians fail to make an impact today is that they do not recognize that the campus is,

4. Ibid., p. 301.
5. Ibid., p. 303.

so far as they are concerned, a mission station. Once, however, they recognize that Christians on the campus are a very small minority, and that they can expect very little assistance, a new day of Christian realism may emerge. We need modern Timothy Dwights, but they cannot operate successfully without arduous preparation, and they cannot operate alone. At no point in our culture are the words of Christ, "Behold, I send you out as lambs in the midst of wolves" (Luke 10:3), more pertinent. We may note that these chilling words are addressed to missionaries, because Christ was sending them out.

Though it is not universally recognized as such, many are aware today that one of the major contemporary mission fields is the membership of the local churches. It can no longer be validly assumed, if it ever could be, that most church members are committed Christians or that they look upon themselves as part of the missionary force. Thousands are only nominal members with very low expectancy of what is required of them. They do a little perfunctory giving; they attend some meetings; they expect help in weddings and funerals. Anyone who has the slightest acquaintance with the New Testament realizes at once how radically this expectation differs from what was originally taught. The major heresy of nominal Christians is to fall back into pre-Christian ways, not remembering that "something greater than the Temple is here" (Matt. 12:6).

It is when we recognize the meaninglessness of much contemporary church membership that we see vividly why it constitutes an important sector of the World Mission field. Church membership is valuable in that it provides a handle. If people claim to be members they can have no valid objection to the effort to evangelize them, since they are rendered intrinsically vulnerable by their own decision to remain in the fellowship. That people want to be counted as members is an indication that their antagonism to the Christian Cause is not complete. While it is right that committed Christians should support foreign mission efforts with money and prayer, it is nevertheless true that, for many of them, the most urgent opportunity involves their fellow members. Great numbers of these admit, when they are frank, that they do not believe in God, that prayer seems to them unreal, and that the stories of Christ, particularly the miracles, are fictitious. They have never subjected their minds with any consistency to a brilliant presentation of the basic faith such as is available in *The Case for Christianity* by C. S. Lewis.[6]

Membership, then, is an invitation to missionary effort, and for that reason we can rightly be grateful that it exists. The committed Christian who sees that he has to be a missionary, if his faith is to be genuine, can start to work at once, without securing the permission of anybody. He can organize study groups, distribute books which have helped him, and develop friendships which, if he is patient, may lead to major decisions. His best opportunities will not come by being precipitous, but by initiating human contacts which may finally lead the other person to make personal inquiries. Knowing that the best witness is the witness of response, he will seek to be ready to provide a clear answer when someone asks him about the hope that is in him (I Pet. 3:15). It ought to be every Christian's responsibility to conduct alone and with others a lay witness mission.

We are amazed, sometimes, when we see how a modest individual, inspired by Christ's example, can give himself to others. One man has, for several years, kept a Bible School

6. This small book is now published as the first part of *Mere Christianity* (New York: The Macmillan Company, 1960).

going in a state mental hospital by encouraging the patients to accept positions of leadership. He stays chiefly in the background, but week after week, year in and year out, he is recruiting teachers, visiting patients, and always engaging in the ministry of friendship. He does not claim to be indispensable, but he knows that nothing of importance occurs, anywhere, unless some persons live continually under the weight of the responsibility.

Valuable as individual effort may be, group work is better. When Christ sent out the first missionary band (Mark 6:7), He sent them not singly, but two by two. There has been a long and productive history of mission work based upon this particular pattern, the individual who feels called often recruiting a companion to go with him. In this way there is the beginning of a fellowship and a consequent transcendence of mere professionalism. In approaching nominal members it is best to try to draw the visited one into the small fellowship of search and witness, which has already been formed, rather than to ask for money, as is naturally expected. In this fashion some seekers may become finders, and nominal members may become committed ones. This enterprise is not easy and there will always be many failures, but the task is one which is obviously self-justifying.

One means of evangelism that has been employed only recently is that in which people are organized into vocational groups. The best successes have been among Christian physicians, though even here relatively little has been accomplished. Some success has been achieved when Christian doctors have formed a redemptive fellowship into which other doctors, previously limited to nominal church membership, have been drawn. It is obvious that if we were to take local missionary work seriously, this is what we should inaugurate among nurses, engineers, broadcasters, and many more. We have here a virtually untapped Christian opportunity for novelty.

The Church of the Saviour, in the nation's capital, has given a strong lead in the direction of group missions. Every member of this remarkable congregation is required to be part of a group, which meets regularly. For several years the groups were primarily prayer groups, with a good deal of mutual sharing of problems and resources. Gordon Cosby, the pastor, later became convinced that the groups could be more effective in every way, including help to one another, if each group had a particular mission, some working with the poor and some with the mentally ill. Here is an exciting pattern which is applicable to the Christian Cause anywhere, regardless of denomination or geography. The appealing vision is that of a Christian Movement in which there is no audience, because all are performers. To become a member of Christ's Church, according to this pattern, is, among other things, to be recruited for the Mission. This, of course, makes membership very demanding and costly, as Christ evidently intended. If not, why did He say, "Whoever does not bear his own cross and come after me, cannot be my disciple"?

As we come near to the end of the twentieth century, looking back on the successes and failures of the Mission during seven dramatic decades, it is important to approach, in complete openness, modern adaptations of what has succeeded in other centuries. It is doubtful if sufficient thought has been given to the creation of new "orders." Orders should be considered because they have been effective, particularly in Roman Catholic mission work. When he wrote his Abingdon prize-winning book, Professor Jaroslav Pelikan made one of his most pertinent observations in this particular connection.

"It was the orders," he said, "that made possible the conversion of Europe, and the absence of anything similar to them has persistently hindered Protestant missions."[7] It was, both Pelikan and Latourette agree, the lack of such orders which postponed the major thrust of Protestant missions until the nineteenth century.

The case for celibate orders on the foreign mission field is clear to the observer as soon as he notes the problems which arise when married couples with children engage in sacrificial work. Though they do not share their parents' call, children are inevitably involved, and it is they who suffer most damage because of the uprootedness of their lives. The visitor can easily see that some of the best work on the foreign field is done by single women who exhibit the beginnings of the kind of order that may be desired. The development of new orders in our generation may provide some dedicated persons with their best chance to do some genuine pioneering.

One of the best by-products of the World Mission is the creation of real contact between supporting fellowships at home and operating fellowships abroad, thereby providing a practical means of transcending provincialism. Some of the most hopeful developments have been secular imitations of the Christian pattern, a fine example being that of Oklahoma State University and its academic counterpart in Ethiopia. Under the provisions of the United States International Technical Assistance Program, called "Point Four," the leaders of the University at Stillwater, Oklahoma, established in the 1950's a sister institution in Ethiopia with primary emphasis upon

7. *The Riddle of Roman Catholicism* (Nashville: Abingdon Press, 1959), p. 88. See also Kenneth Scott Latourette, *Three Centuries of Advance*, Vol. III in A History of the Expansion of Christianity series (New York: Harper & Row, 1939), p. 26.

agriculture, and patterned after the Land-Grant College system of the United States. Though the program was government sponsored, it was in essence a people-to-people project, and while this was not designated officially as mission work, it was the missionary idea which gave the project its major impetus. It is no accident that the chief architects of this program were themselves committed Christians who, without the employment of specifically Christian language, and without any need to introduce it, understood that they were being yoked together with those of a different culture in one phase of Operation Liberation.[8]

Though many are unaware of it, a new development in missionary activity has come to pass in the employment of a great number of short-term missionaries. A committed Christian with a particular skill volunteers for a limited period, with no thought of permanent residence. His specialized work may be that of industrial management, agriculture, or politics. The expectation is that such a recruit will make his contribution and then go on, having sought to render himself unnecessary. The *New York Times* refers to such people as a "New Breed of American Missionary."[9]

One practical application of the exciting idea that Christ has as many potential ambassadors as the Church has members is the recruitment of a vast company of hitherto unenlisted foreign missionaries. Serious acceptance of this idea would produce a radical alteration of pattern in the World Mission, including a change in the financial picture. There is a constant stream of businessmen who leave the United States to represent the great corporations, such as those which deal in oil, in

8. See *Oklahoma State University in Ethiopia*, Terminal Report 1952-1968 (Stillwater, Okla., 1969).
9. See *New York Times*, July 26, 1971, p. 27.

rubber, and in steel. Some of these, there is good reason to know, are church members, and among these are some who are truly committed Christians. Why not find a way to enable these people to carry out their double vocation, joining in one journey or one period of residence both professional and religious responsibilities?[10]

Here is one of the greatest of relatively untapped missionary resources. Besides the business representatives, there are also thousands of government officials, teachers, and agents of foundations. Because most of these, if they could be recruited for Christian work wherever they happen to go, would require no financial assistance for travel or for maintenance, their recruitment would liberate funds, now allocated to other purposes, for the direct needs of impoverished people. The dream, of course, like any worthwhile one, involves a vast amount of work, organization, and training, but however difficult these may prove to be, it is something that can be done. A start has already been made in Washington, D.C., under the inspired leadership of Francis B. Sayre, Dean of the Washington Cathedral. Washington is a natural location for the training of the nonprofessional mission corps, since so many who may be enlisted are foreign service workers employed by the government.

As we contemplate an idea of this magnitude, we soon see that the men and women thus enlisted would gain by it, as would the people whom they would teach and serve in various lands. Under the present system a few committed Christians living abroad become members of English-language churches where they serve for longer or shorter periods. For example,

10. For a presentation of the idea of the involvement of lay missionaries, see David M. Stowe, *Ecumenicity and Evangelism* (Grand Rapids: William B. Eerdmans Publishing Co., 1970), pp. 71 f.

there is a church in Hong Kong in which most of the members are Americans and in which the congregation operates very much as it would if it were in North America. Though the experience is helpful, it involves little of the conception of the nonprofessional Mission. The radical alternative to the familiar pattern of members as primarily attenders is for the Christians living away from home to be organized into a conscious missionary band. The wonderful thing is that they do not need to be "sent," for they are already there!

If the lay missionary conception is to be effective, a great deal of education will be required. The persons enlisted will require new and specialized training in the meaning of the Gospel and its diffusion. Some of this can go on before the workers leave their own communities, but more will have to be continued under the direction of professional missionaries after the lay workers reach their new homes. Because grown people can learn very rapidly when there is a practical motivation for learning, representatives of secular enterprises can, if they take the task seriously, become conversant, in their spare time, with the essentials of Christian thought. For many of these, such a use of time may be a welcome relief from the constant round of cocktail parties which often mark the lives of Americans living abroad who spend too much of their time with their fellow nationals.

The employment of nonprofessional missionaries in large numbers can be a genuine breakthrough, but it will not become this unless the persons involved are made to feel the excitement of a great idea. The great idea is that the Christian Society is intended to be leaven, that the purpose of the leaven is the penetration of the world, and that the leaven resides in the general membership. Once it is widely understood that a person, by becoming a member of the Church, automatically becomes a missionary wherever he is, the preparation for a major victory will already have been made.

One variant of the idea of the nonprofessional missionary force is that of the tentmaking ministry. This term arises from the practice of the Apostle Paul in supporting himself by making tents at the same time that he was then the world's most famous missionary. We know that he stayed, in Corinth, at the home of Aquila and Priscilla and that he stayed there because they were also tentmakers (Acts 18:3). Partly as a result of the increasing difficulty of raising funds for the foreign program, and partly because of its own inherent advantages, Christians in many developing countries are now encouraged to earn their support in secular occupations at the same time that they serve the Christian Cause. One of the major advantages of such a system is that it builds up self-respect among new Christians. Without some such plan, there is a strong tendency for new Christians to become too dependent upon the financial assistance which the boards are expected to provide.

The tentmaking ministry may, in the long run, be even more appropriate on the home front than on the foreign field. That clergymen of Western lands are in real trouble there is no doubt, though many of them appear not to recognize the revolution that is taking place. We are clearly witnessing in America the rise of anticlericalism, from which, in the past, we have been relatively free. Certainly there is, in many denominations, and especially in those in which the clergy have seemed to be overeager to politicize the faith, a real tension between the clergy and the laity. In many situations the clergy seem so far removed from reality that they are unaware of their unpopularity. Because few of them have ever met a payroll or have had to account in detail for the use of their time, they are looked upon with decreasing respect.

The Christian who, on the one hand, accepts pastoral leadership and, on the other, earns his living in a factory or office, may represent the pattern of future Christian service which will finally succeed better than any other. His secular earning which frees him from dependence upon the contributions of the members makes possible a relationship of mutual self-respect. With the contemporary shortness of the work week, there is plenty of free time for an employed man to study and to counsel, provided he disciplines himself in regard to time and recognizes that it is precious. Above all, the person who fills this dual role avoids the suspicion, in his own and in other minds, that he is an economic parasite. Also, he transcends the conventional pattern of the official holy man, skilled in the performance of sacred rites, but not one who is pulling his weight in the world.

The financial advantages of a new pattern of secularized ministry may be enormous. The common practice is to keep adding to the staff on the unsupported supposition that this will bring strength. Often the exact opposite is the result, because the proliferation of staff relieves too many of the members of their own religious responsibilities. In short, members feel that they do not need to be missionaries themselves, because they have hired others to do this work.

Always, if we take the idea of the Universal Mission seriously, we must watch for unused human resources, because we are not rich enough to waste any. One of the major resources now largely unexploited is that of retired persons. In our present commercial society, the shortening of the work week is matched by the advancement of retirement to an earlier age. Consequently, an extended period of time is available for noncommercial employment. While some find that their retirement pay or social security is not sufficient for the cost of living and therefore seek paid employment after official retirement, there are many others who, with some care in management of funds, can be liberated entirely, for long periods, from the necessity of earning.

What the Church must do for retired Christians, if it is to accept the missionary conception of membership, is to equip people to make the retired years into years of glorious opportunity for service. For the committed Christian, retirement means not an introduction to nothingness, but liberation for service. If this idea is to be effective, we must begin preparation for liberation long before it occurs, because, if we wait, it may already be too late. That the idea is beginning to catch on is deeply encouraging. Recently, a man said, half-jokingly, "I am going as a missionary to Florida." Whether the freedom from toil, which modern technology makes possible, is a blessing or a curse depends, in large measure, upon the pattern of thinking about ourselves and our vocations. It is here that the Christian faith can make some of its most potent contributions. The man who always wanted to be a missionary, but could not do so, he thought, because of the demands of family and secular occupation, may bring deep meaning to his mature years by volunteering to engage in work for which there is no financial support. Assuming good health, which is increasingly experienced after the age of retirement, new and hitherto unsuspected avenues may open. Thereby the Christian Movement may again demonstrate its genius for the creation of novelty.

Once we accept the idea that the field is the world, we change the whole image of the Mission. Much of the problem arises from the gratuitous assumption that the missionary is necessarily a clergyman and a man devoid of skills in common life, thus representing a pattern which is almost sure to seem obsolete in the modern world. But if we realize that missionary merely means any follower of Christ who takes his faith seriously, the whole undertaking is revolutionized.

An effort has been made to convince Christians that they are "ministers," whatever their occupation, but success in this effort is far from complete. People still speak of the clergyman as "the minister" which, of course, eliminates themselves from a similar function, since the definite article is intrinsically singular. While the change in semantics in regard to the sharp distinction between minister and lay Christian may be virtually impossible at this time, there appears to be a different situation in regard to the concept of Mission. In any case, this is an area of hope. If wide exposure is given to the idea that the Mission is essential to the Christian Cause and that it recognizes neither geographical nor professional limitations, a start has been made on the road to renewal.

5

The Theology of Mission

The Church exists by mission as fire exists by burning.

EMIL BRUNNER

The Church of Jesus Christ does not *have missions*; in its very life it *is Mission*. The recognition of this has been one of the remarkable theological developments of the recent past, a development which is shared equally by Protestants and Roman Catholics. Brunner's epigram about the fire has had the effect, not of adding a new idea, but of bringing a number of scattered ideas into a single pattern of meaning. The basic metaphor, that expressed in Luke 12:49, has come to mean more in our time than it has meant for generations: "I came to cast fire upon the earth; and would that it were already kindled!" There is marked agreement that, just as the fire which ceases to burn becomes nothing, so the Church which is satisfied to hug its treasures to itself is no longer genuine. The Church must become an Incendiary Fellowship.

Missionary action, like any good thing, can be easily misunderstood by outsiders or perverted by insiders. There is, almost always, the danger that Mission may appear to be little more than religious imperialism. Even the language Christians have used may contribute to confusion at this point. Sometimes it seems that Christians wish to expand in order to glorify their own religion or to extend their power over other minds. One illustration of this particular danger is provided by the words of Charles Clayton Morrison, long editor of *The Christian Century*. "The enterprise of Christian missions," he wrote, "is the expression of the expansive impulse of Christianity."[1] Of course, Dr. Morrison was not defending mere expansion, but, because there is a strong temptation to interpret events in this fashion, careful attention to the theology of Mission is of crucial importance.

The chief motive for the Christian Mission is best expressed in a paradox, which is the central paradox of the Gospel. We soon notice, as we study Christ's own words about the Church, that He employed a number of metaphors, of which the one about the fire is the most striking. He spoke of "salt," of "light," and of "leaven." At first glance these seem to be very different from one another, but, as we examine them, we soon realize that they have one feature in common: *all are figures representing penetration*. The salt exists to penetrate the meat, the light exists to penetrate the darkness, and the leaven exists to penetrate the dough in order that it may rise. Each is lost, yet is, at the same time, creative of something of supreme value. The most surprising fact is that each of these is frustrated in its true function whenever it is *saved*, because the essence of each is that it is radically expendable. The way to destroy the usefulness of a lamp is to try to protect it by putting it under a meal-tub (Matt. 5:15, NEB). What we do not use we really lose!

---

1. *What is Christianity?* (Chicago: Willett, Clark & Co., 1940), p. 300.

The central paradox about saving and losing provides the Christian Mission with its *raison d'être*. The paradox appears in all of the Synoptic Gospels, the basic statement being, "For whoever would save his life will lose it; and whoever loses his life for my sake and the gospel's will save it" (Mark 8:35). Herein lies the essence of the theology which has made the phenomenon of Mission possible. Christianity, as has often been said, is, by its very nature, diffusive, but the doctrine of diffusion does not stand alone; it follows logically from the doctrine of expendability.

When the doctrine of expendability is fully accepted, it becomes at once obvious that, in contrast to many organizations, the Church is not instituted for the benefit of its members. Christ enlists ordinary men and women into His enduring fellowship, not primarily in order to save them, but because He has work for them to do. It is a genuine revelation that His primary call to commitment, "Come to me," is associated at once with a call to labor, "Take my yoke upon you." The Church is essential to the Christian, not because it brings him personal advancement or even inspiration, but because, with all its failures, it is an indispensable instrument for the redemption of the world.

Here is a sufficient answer to anyone who asks the reason for the missionary enterprise. Mission is not extracurricular, but represents the essential meaning of the Church as a unique fellowship. Because the Church is meant to be a healing, lifting, and therefore a redemptive fellowship, the Mission is not something which is added as an extra. Devoid of Mission it is possible to have a successful institution which provides services to its members and attenders, but it is not the Church. Dr. DeWolf's answer on this point is strong and clear. "If it be asked," he says, "why there should be a Christian mission, it may be replied that the mission is of the very nature of the Christian faith and so of the Church."[2] When we speak of the love of Christ, this is what we mean; it is love of this kind which gives itself without limit, without self-seeking, and even without hope of reward. By this high standard, of course, many churches reveal their lack of authenticity. They build monuments to themselves, and they have their reward; they spend more money for their own welfare than for that of others. Each such failure is painful, but what is really wonderful is that the standard of the shared life has never, in spite of repeated failures, been wholly lost. It is a constantly failing Church that has kept intact the pattern of thought by which its own self-criticism is made possible.

Much of the theology of Mission is centered in the theology of the Church. All observers note that, as soon as missionaries arrive in new fields, infant congregations are formed. Though they might not put it in exactly this way, they realize that, for the Christian, there is no reality without community. Each missionary sooner or later verifies the prophetic words on this point which were uttered by John Baillie. "I cannot," he said, "be a Christian all by myself. I cannot retire into my own shell or into my own corner and live the Christian life there. A single individual cannot be a Christian in his singleness."[3] People are helped most by being drawn into a redemptive fellowship of others who, like themselves, are obviously imperfect, yet are partners in both commitment and caring. If we look for the pure fellowship we shall look in vain, but the impure human fellowship, centered in Christ, is miraculous in

2. L. Harold DeWolf, in *Christian Mission in Theological Perspective*, ed. by Gerald H. Anderson (Nashville: Abingdon Press, 1967), p. 49.

3. *Invitation to Pilgrimage* (New York: Charles Scribner's Sons, 1945), p. 119.

its effect. To an astonishing degree, it has provided men and women with a sense of personal dignity which otherwise they would not have known.

The metaphors of penetration help us to understand why it is not absurd for the Christian Church to see itself as the prime instrument in the creation of a more humane civilization. It is here, indeed, that we observe a remarkable combination of humility and boldness. "Missions make the claim," wrote Hendrik Kraemer, "that Christianity contains the forces of moral and spiritual regeneration, so sorely needed in this time of disintegration."[4] If the reader discounts the words of Dr. Kraemer, a Dutch theologian, on the ground that he had a professional stake in his bold claim, the confirming words of a lay thinker may be helpful. All who have loved the now-famous autobiography of Lord Tweedsmuir must have noted the Christian emphasis with which the statesman-scholar man of letters brought his book to an end. "There have been," he wrote, "high civilizations in the past which have not been Christian, but in the world as we know it I believe that civilization must have a Christian basis, and must ultimately rest on the Christian Church."[5]

Lord Tweedsmuir's claim does not seem extreme when we realize that Christianity provides that combination of the dignity of the individual and compassion for the poor and oppressed which is precisely what a better civilization requires. The personal dignity comes from the realization that not a sparrow falls without the Father (Matt. 10:29), while the emphasis on compassion comes because each is called as

4. *The Christian Message in a Non-Christian World* (New York: Harper & Brothers, 1938), p. 436.
5. *Pilgrim's Way; An Essay in Recollection* (Cambridge: The Riverside Press, 1940), p. 297.

Christ's recruit to share in the liberation mentioned in Luke 4:18-19.

If this combination is found in any other pattern of thought, we do not know where it is. Christianity, in its essence, is neither a ceremonial system nor an ecclesiastical hierarchy, but a vision of universal dignity for mankind. It encourages a way of life in which leaders are servants (Mark 10:45), and in which the way to be truly a child of God is to be a peacemaker (Matt. 5:9).

The Mission is many things, but it cannot succeed unless those who operate it learn the difference between what is primary and what is secondary. This was understood clearly by William Temple in what may turn out to be the best publicized Christian address of the twentieth century, when he referred to "the great new fact of our era." This was his enthronement address in Canterbury Cathedral on St. George's Day, 1942. By the great new fact the Archbishop meant the emergence of the world Christian fellowship. Here was the ecumenical dream coming true and being celebrated even during dark days with three more years of war yet to endure. In spite of all of his devotion to Christian union, Temple saw union as primarily a byproduct, rather than something at which to aim directly. His words on a noble occasion are so important that they deserve widespread dissemination long after his death.

> As though in preparation for such a time as this, God has been building up a Christian fellowship which now extends into almost every nation, and binds citizens of them all together in true unity and natural love. No human agency has planned this. It is the result of the great missionary enterprise of the last one hundred and fifty years. Neither the missionaries nor those who sent them out were

aiming at the creation of a world-wide fellowship inter-
penetrating the nations, bridging the gulfs between them,
and supplying the promise of a check to their rivalries. The
aim for nearly the whole period was to preach the Gospel
to as many individuals as could be reached so that those
who were won to discipleship should be put in the way of
eternal salvation. Almost incidentally the great world-fel-
lowship has arisen; it is the great new fact of our era.[6]

We have, from the beginning of modern missions to peoples
in undeveloped lands, faced the problem of where to start.
Shall we start with the effort to change the civilization, as in
the establishment of schools and hospitals, or shall we start
with the Gospel message? Even after we have agreed on the
need of both, the question of temporal priority still remains.
We are fortunate today to have the careful answer of a sea-
soned missionary in the words of Bishop Neill:

> After more than a century it is possible on purely em-
> pirical grounds to pronounce a judgment on the two meth-
> ods. Experience has shown that the order of priority must
> always be first conversion and then social change; if the
> inner transformation has been brought about, the problem
> of social change and uplift can be tackled with far greater
> prospects of success. The old principle of the Gospel "Seek
> ye first the kingdom of God and his righteousness, and all
> these things shall be added unto you," has proved itself to
> be not a remote and distant ideal but the most practical of
> advice.[7]

The sharing of the Gospel is the first aim, but much else
follows by consequence. The experience of unity among

6. *The Church Looks Forward* (New York: The Macmillan Company,
1944), p. 2.
7. Op. cit., p. 56.

Christians is one of these, and a multitude of social services is another. If we do not start with what is primary, we are not likely to achieve what is secondary, for this is a resultant. If we try to maintain the far-flung social services, without the concern for the central message, the day may come when the services will be impossible because the central motivation will have been lost. The call to become fishers of men precedes the call to wash one another's feet.

Unfortunately, the polarization of our generation extends even to the missionary enterprise, each party looking disparagingly at the work of the other. Thus, it is common to hear some speak scornfully of "soul saving," while others speak, with equal condescension, of "activism." The clear answer is that both are needed and that they will always be needed. Each person requires a faith to give him stability in the midst of confusion as he requires what hospitals and schools can provide. There is a clear decline whenever we try to maintain either of these apart from the other. On the mission field, more than anywhere else, the roots and the fruits must be held together.

That Christ taught the necessity of wholeness is beyond doubt. How dare we choose between concern for the present life and concern for the life everlasting, when Christ obviously emphasized both! To say that, since our only concern is to feed a man now, we are not interested in his eternal future, is to be superficial in the extreme, while to be concerned for his soul without reference to his broken and diseased body is to forget the Christian emphasis upon healing. Always the message is "These you ought to have done, without neglecting the others" (Matt. 23:23). There is no Gospel without Mission and there is no Mission without message.

It has been common practice in the recent past, even among Christian leaders, to speak critically of the motto initiated by John R. Mott, "The evangelization of the world in this generation." The criticism arises from the supposed naïveté of entertaining unrealistic hopes, the phrase being often dragged into discussions for the purpose of finding something to ridicule. But if there is any naïveté, it is that which is demonstrated by the scorners themselves. Neither Dr. Mott nor any of his close associates ever underestimated the barriers to the extension of Christ's Kingdom nor did they speak of the "conversion" of the world in one generation. They made, indeed, an important distinction between evangelization and conversion. Conversion is something which is certainly beyond our power to accomplish, but evangelism is a task which, with all of our weakness, we are able to perform. Much of our difficulty lies in the popular understanding about what evangelism is. David Stowe has been helpful in his definition of evangelism. "Evangelism," he has written, "is the act of so presenting the gospel of God which is revealed in Christ that men are persuaded to commit themselves to his purpose."[8]

That doors are closed temporarily does not mean that they will be closed permanently. Indeed, there is already a thawing of icy relations so far as China is concerned. It is wholly possible that many who are now alive may live to see new chapters in the World Mission which today seem virtually impossible. Certainly, the external features of life will change markedly in almost every part of the globe, and technological changes are unpredictable, but the needs of the human heart are independent of both social and technological revolution.

8. *Ecumenicity and Evangelism*, op. cit., pp. 19, 20.

Because the demand for meaning and the demand for fellowship have been amazingly constant, there must be evangelization in every generation.

In the intellectual problem of missions, there is one major key to a solution, the *idea of witness*. By emphasis upon witness, it is possible to bridge the gap between message and service, between word and deed, and between the roots and fruits of the Christian faith. One of the first of Christian thinkers to see this was Hendrik Kraemer, who said that the reason why a missionary must perform social services and also preach is that both of these are forms of the same fundamental function, that of witnessing. "All activities of the Christian Church and all missions in social service, in education, in medical work, and in so many things more only get their right missionary foundation and perspective if they belong as intrinsically to the category of witness as preaching or evangelization."[9]

With witness as the theological key to the puzzle we quickly see how to overcome the either-or mentality. After all, the idea of being a witness is both the alpha and the omega of the practical Gospel. In a profound sense, the entire Christian Church is meant to be nothing more nor less than a Fellowship of Witnesses.

We need to help one another to know how to be faithful witnesses. We must, of course, try to make our lives speak, but in all humility we recognize that this is not sufficient, because our lives are never good enough. Possibly no one has helped readers to see the necessity of witnesses more than has Gabriel Marcel, whose essay on the subject is widely

9. Op. cit., p. 433.

known.[10] The Christian, Marcel taught, is free in many ways, but he is not free to be silent. If he has found a center of stability in his life, and if he is aware of the confusion and perplexity about him, it is required morally that he speak by word or deed and preferably by both together.

The greatest danger in modern missions is not the one which existed previously, that of evangelism without service, but rather that of service without evangelism. If the service is performed as nothing but service, i.e., without being done as witnesses, it is bound to wither and die, for a fragmented Christianity is always close to death. Because the service which is not grounded in a message will soon cease to be even a service, the important strategy lies both in performing the service and in understanding the reason for it; if it stands alone it will soon cease to stand at all. Perhaps Kraemer's most helpful observation was on this exact point. "The social and cultural activity of the Church," he wrote, "are not accessories to its essential programme of witness and proclamation of the Gospel, but expressions of its nature."[11]

The more that witness can be understood, the better for the World Mission. Witness, like other essentials of Christian theology, involves paradox and is at first mystifying. Though witness is profoundly unselfish, it must, in the nature of things, employ the first person singular. All realize that the witness of a man in court is worthless if he merely reports hearsay; he must tell what he has experienced personally. In the end, all that a poor man can say, if he wants to go beyond speculation, is "Whereas I was blind, now I see," for there

10. *The Philosophy of Existence* (New York: Philosophical Library, 1949), p. 68.
11. Op. cit., p. 433.

is no way to go behind this in a courtroom or anywhere else. At the same time, however, the center of reference is not self, but Another. Though the man who engages in witness speaks on the basis of firsthand personal experience, it is not of himself that he speaks. The witnessing Christian speaks *of Christ*, and he speaks *to others*, who need what he has to report.

In the last earthly words attributed to Christ, the word which we translate as "witness" is the same word from which we derive the word "martyr." This particular Greek word is translated three times in the New Testament as "martyr" and twenty-nine times as "witness." It is significant that those who engage in the act of witness are thereby made vulnerable. In extreme cases, there is the danger of death, but more often the danger is merely that of ridicule or neglect. It is good that all who know that the Christian is inevitably called to be a missionary should also know that, even in our time, the price is high and the road is rough. Any religion which is marked primarily by peace of mind is bound to be spurious. Certainly, we are in the wrong place when all men speak well of us.

The kind of theology which we espouse makes an enormous difference in the effectiveness of the Mission. As we observe the mission field around the world, we conclude that at least two kinds of theology are failing in this generation. One of these is the old-fashioned Fundamentalism and the other is the old-fashioned Liberalism. The former fails because it cannot meet the challenge of scientific thinking and the latter fails because it is too broad and syncretistic to have a cutting edge. But while these are failing, there is a third kind of thinking which is really powerful and which avoids the pitfalls of both the right and the left. It is the part of wisdom to examine this third way and to try to understand why it is winning so many minds.

It was generally agreed at the Urbana student conference, which reached its high point on January 1, 1971, that the most effective single interpreter of the Gospel there was John Stott. This man, who is unknown to millions of Americans, is more successful than are most Christian leaders today in reaching the minds and hearts of young people. He is Vicar of All Souls' Church, Langham Place, in the West End of London. Keeping loyally to the forms of worship of the Anglican Communion, John Stott is able, at the same time, to be evangelistic in mood. Often on Sunday nights the large and dignified building at the end of Regent Street is packed with people, the majority being under twenty-five years of age, many of whom become recruits for the Christian Cause and, consequently, missionaries in the wilderness of London. What is striking to the visitor living for some time in London is that the average church building is nearly empty, not only on Sunday nights, but on Sunday mornings as well. The intelligent person will do all that he can to find out why Stott's ministry is so much more effective than is the ministry exercised at most other places.

At first it is hard to see the secret of John Stott's strength. He employs no sensational tricks and his message is entirely straightforward, seemingly lacking in emotional appeal. His message conforms to the title of one of his books, *Basic Christianity*, his appeal, over and over, being not only both Biblical and rational, but above all, Christ-centered. As we analyze what this man says, it appears to be very simple. He has a strong Christian belief and he expresses it unapologetically, with no concession to passing fashions. He believes that God really is, that He is like Christ, that He cares for every soul, that there is a life everlasting, and that the Bible is a trustworthy guide because it is divinely inspired. But why would this attract people of all ages? Isn't this old stuff?

The answer to this question becomes clear when we realize the degree to which a modern metropolis is a genuine mission field. People attend All Souls' Church and listen with rapt attention, partly because they are hearing a message which they literally have never heard before. This includes many who have had some church connections. The truth is that in many churches the kind of Basic Christianity which Stott preaches has not been heard at all in the recent past. Instead, there are lectures on social issues with boring regularity, and often the speakers emphasize their doubts more than their convictions. To hear an obviously educated man say that he believes that God is like Christ is really shocking because it is essentially novel. A long dry spell makes even a modest rain a thrilling experience.

In the Mission to modern man it is belief that makes the difference. Telling people to be good or kind or tolerant will not change many lives, but confrontation with Christ, based upon the conviction that He provides people of all generations with the one solid point of their experience, is a different matter entirely. The more than eleven thousand young people who met at Urbana had all of the same culture as their contemporaries, with one exception, this exception having to do with belief. If we do not try to learn something from this we are being willfully blind.

The simplicity that we seek is that of a goal and not of a beginning. The Christian Mission does not begin in simplicity, because each honest recruit has his own doubts, and sometimes his despair, but these are not final. That marvelous missionary, George Fox, reported in his *Journal* his revolutionary insight that, while there is "an ocean of darkness and death," there is also "an ocean of light and love that flows over the ocean of darkness." Maturity in Christian experience comes, not by denying the difficulties, but by discovering a personal commitment which transcends them. The ultimate simplicity of conviction is what C. S. Lewis called "a costly distillation."

The question, "What do you think of the Christ?" (Matt. 22:42) is the crucial one for the Mission. The probability is that the majority of people, at least in the West, who think of Christ at all, think of Him as a Teacher and only a teacher. Having never really read the Gospels for themselves, they suppose that He went about advocating love and not much else. What must be seen with clarity is that if Christ is Teacher, and only Teacher, He is not able to provide the motivation for Mission which is desperately needed. Men require not merely a person to whom they can listen, but One to whom they can be committed and for whom they can become ambassadors. Because the task is intrinsically arduous, something more than the teacher-student relationship is required.

Over and over we are told today that we must become more "human," but the meaning of this exhortation is far from clear. There are, unfortunately, many different ways of being human. It is human to seek power over others; it is human to maneuver for our own interests; it is human to be a tyrant. Men differ, generically, from all beasts, but the difference is not that men are naturally good. While human behavior may be far more noble than that of any animal, it may also be far more vindictive in its calculated cruelty. To a degree which is not represented in any other creature, man is indeterminate.

Herein lies the inadequacy of all humanism. Men call them-selves humanists, sometimes, when they cease to believe that God is, but they almost always end by sounding pathetic. If they say, modishly, that they believe in *people*, there is no escape from sentimentality. After all, the Nazis were people. Many beliefs are vulnerable to attack, but the belief in natu-ral human goodness is worse than vulnerable; it is indefensi-ble. Many of the people whom the Christian missionary seeks to serve are disappointing people, and some of them are obviously ungrateful. Unless we have something as powerful as the love of Christ, the attempted human service is not likely to endure.

In addition to what is popularly known as humanism, and in contrast to it, there has long been recognized a Christian Humanism. This term has been employed because commit-ment to Christ means not less attention to human beings, but more. It is, in many instances, a Christ-centered faith that has contributed to great advances in human welfare, liberation from slavery being a striking example of this. By Christian Humanism is meant the emphasis upon the importance of persons in contrast to the importance of things. Christ is the Christian's object of supreme commitment, but the chief external evidence of this commitment is service to the breth-ren. Feeding the hungry is not the center of the Christian's faith, but it provides, nevertheless, a verification of that faith. Those who do not show compassion to the brethren are none of His.

The life of compassion is part of the fruit, but belief be-longs to the root, without which the fruit withers and finally ceases to appear at all. It is popularly supposed, in the modern world, that theology is a dull subject without practical sig-nificance, but this is a serious mistake in judgment. Unless the theology is straight, nothing else will be straight, for life is lost without meaning, however competent men may be in particular sciences, and however skilled in their vocations. Men need many things, including bread, but it is recorded in both the Old Testament and the New that they cannot live by bread alone (Deut. 8:3, Luke 4:4). If we really care about people, we must try to provide them with what they need most. Theology is simply Greek for "the knowledge of God" and, if we have even a little of this, it is our duty to share it.

Fortunately, there is a theology developing in our generation which meets the qualifications which the support of the World Mission requires. While there is no single name for this theology, we are not far wrong if we refer to it as Rational Evangelicalism. Wherever this is seriously espoused it meets human need as the alternatives on both the left and the right are not able to do.

It is necessary at this point in Christian history to recognize that while there may be variations on the fringes, there must be at the center an irreducible minimum of conviction. Whether Christians have bishops or not is relatively trivial, and many other matters of discussion are in the same category. We shall be far stronger if we know what is peripheral and what is central. For example, whether we have communion with Christ is of supreme significance, but whether this is done by the use of bread and wine, or without them, is a matter in which honest differences do no harm. "Our communion with Christ is and ought to be our greatest and chiefest work" was written by a scholarly man[12] who did not make use of physical elements at all. In a similar fashion,

12. Robert Barclay, *Apology for the True Christian Divinity*, 1678, Proposition XIII, v.

the question of how to be baptized is peripheral, but *whether* a man is really immersed in the love of Christ is central.

It is easy to imagine a situation in which the Christian faith might become so diluted that it would eventually lose its original character altogether. Indeed, such a development has actually occurred in some of the religions which we study. Fortunately, Christianity has the incalculably valuable asset of the New Testament, which includes noble affirmations like that of Romans 8:38-39:

> For I am sure that neither death, nor life, nor angels, nor principalities, nor things present, nor things to come, nor height, nor depth, nor anything else in all creation, will be able to separate us from the love of God in Christ Jesus our Lord.

If these affirmations should be abandoned, the shell might survive for awhile, but the living kernel would be gone. Some ceremonies, such as those connected with marriage and death, might continue for a considerable time, for such celebrations are consistent with a decadent religion, but it is hard to imagine the continuation of the Mission with its demands for personal sacrifice. Sharing will finally cease if there is nothing to share.

There are a few cardinal points which we dare not abandon or even minimize. The main points are that Christ is trustworthy, that God really is and is like Him, that prayer is genuine, that miracle is possible, and that the death of the flesh does not separate us from the divine attention. If any of these should be seriously modified, as would be the case if God were to be thought of as an impersonal force, what has been known as Christianity would be at an end. Its successor, by whatever name, would finally be unrecognizably different.

There is no way to exaggerate the potential strength of a ministry which combines evangelical theology with fearless mentality and a genuine concern for people. Those who settle for emphasis upon liturgy or activism or detached intellectuality are missing a marvelous opportunity. The Christian leadership that can make a real difference in our time, and the time immediately ahead, will combine the Christ-centeredness of Samuel Shoemaker with the tough rationality of C. S. Lewis and the social realism of Reinhold Niebuhr. What is really foolish is to suppose that this combination is an impossible dream. The union of such qualities is possible because they are in no sense incompatible. All readers already know some persons who approximate the required combination of emphases, and consequently realize that here is where power is to be found. One reason for the continued admiration for the late John Baillie is the degree to which he approached the effective combination just described.

The more we emphasize the basic theology of Mission the more we are prepared for beneficent self-criticism. One of our greatest mistakes today is that of supporting too much overhead. We build up a religious bureaucracy which tends to proliferate in something of the manner with which we are familiar in governments. The remote mission station, where humble people serve other people for the love of Christ, is a place of wonder, but few would describe missionary head-quarters in this fashion. Unfortunately, it is possible for a mission board and its professional officers to be almost completely out of touch with the rank and file of the membership whom they supposedly represent and who contribute the funds. This is especially the case when the officials seem to be more concerned with exerting political pressure than they are with evangelism.

Another serious mistake is that of commissioning persons for work in home universities or on the foreign field who do not have a conscious commitment to Christ. It is possible to find persons in both of these areas who are pleased to be employed and who render some services, but who, at the same time, have no unapologetic witness to make. Some reject the whole idea of winning men and women to Christ and reveal no motivation which distinguishes them from the ordinary Peace Corps worker. These may be good people, but they cannot provide the leadership necessary to guide the World Mission into the magnitude which alone can justify its existence. Boards need to be far more careful in selecting personnel, for, in the long run, persons are all that count. Much of the missionary equipment may be taken over by government, but that will not, by any means, spell the end of the Mission if it is staffed by humble, committed people who serve primarily because they care.

If we understand the deepest reason for the Mission, we soon realize that this process of secularization need not be construed as a threat. It is not conceivable that the evangelical message, which brought the missions into existence in the first place, will ever become the responsibility of any government. The more, then, that stress is placed upon the deepest reason for the Mission, the more will it be understood why it cannot be outmoded. But what if most people refuse to listen? That will not stop the Mission, for rejection has occurred before. The Christian simply goes on, and finally some persons will listen again. "Most men's love will grow cold," we are assured, "but he who endures to the end will be saved" (Matt. 24:12-13).

"Apostle" and "missionary" are synonymous words, both referring to those who are impelled to share what they greatly prize. Though both can refer to those who are professionally employed, this reference is not exhaustive, for they can also refer to millions of persons who are engaged in secular and domestic pursuits. The intelligent Christian strategy is not that of denying or even of lowering the ministry, but rather that of enlarging and universalizing it. It is by the recovery of the dignity of the Mission, and in no other way, that the grand conception of the Universal Apostolate can be approached in practice.

The achievement of the Universal Apostolate ought to be the major practical objective of local Christian congregations anywhere. The local church, when it understands its vocation, exists primarily to prepare its members for participation in the mission at a multitude of points. Robert Raines feels this so keenly that he prints his conclusion on this subject in italics. "Every local church," he says, "needs to define its own mission fields and appraise its congregational program in terms of its effectiveness or irrelevance to the task of equipping its people for mission."[13] Raines describes the chief fields for ordinary Christians, listing them as (1) family, (2) work, and (3) community. "Much of the world," he says, "thinks it knows what the Church is like and has dismissed it as irrelevant to the currents of modern history and, worse, irredeemably dull! We must find new ways of being the Church in the world so as to surprise the world."[14]

The worldwide Christian fellowship is one of the miracles of history, providing a more powerful human bond than is known in any other connection. It is not necessary to minimize its failures or to deny the ineptitude of Christ's human

13. *Reshaping the Christian Life* (New York: Harper & Row, 1964), p. 41.
14. Ibid., p. 47.

agents. Blindness, selfishness, divisiveness, and stupidity have appeared, but, nevertheless, since the miracle has occurred, there is excellent reason to believe that it will continue. Those who assume that religion is a spent force are advised to think again, for strange as it may be, religion seems to die in some places, only to emerge in others. We never know how or where the emergence of spiritual novelty will appear, but, if history is any guide, it will come again and yet again. Christians are always a minority, and they are often ignored, but the Kingdom of Christ can bear a long drought.

Much of the secret of the miracle lies in the fact that the apostle in every age speaks not of himself, but of Another. Missionaries are not sent to advertise their own inventions, productions, or achievements.

> We do not go in order to spread "our Religion," or "our values," not even to share our best. For it would indeed be preposterous if we thought that our religion and culture would necessarily be of benefit to the whole wide world. And those to whom we come would rightly object to our superiority complex if we came because our religion was better than theirs. The whole situation is changed, however, if we go to speak of the God whom we have not invented or created, but whom we have come to know as the Lord of life and whose reign we must announce because it has been announced to us.[15]

As I end this book, I think of a Sunday morning in an African township outside Johannesburg. We gathered for worship, with our bodies very close to one another, because the room was filled. Most of the attenders were black people,

---

15. W. A. Visser 't Hooft, *None Other Gods* (New York: Harper & Brothers, 1937), p. 40.

but color seemed utterly unimportant that morning. Some of us did not know the language in which hymns were sung and prayers were uttered, but that made no difference at all. We understood where the words came from, and we were drawn together because, in spirit, we were looking in the same direction. Translation would have seemed impertinent, and the affection was so obvious that it did not require mention. What a marvelous faith it is that can penetrate into the heart of the Transvaal and there provide a deeper basis of fellowship than is possible in any secular situation in that troubled land. We knew that we were observing something of genuine wonder, and also something which will endure, for the Kingdom of Christ is potentially coextensive with the inhabited world. If people ever settle on another planet, it will extend there, also.

72 73 74 75 10 9 8 7 6 5 4 3 2 1